AF683086

The Constitution of Public Philosophy

Toward a Synthesis of Freedom and Responsibility in Postmodern America

E. Robert Statham, Jr.

IRVINE SULLIVAN INGRAM LIBRARY
STATE UNIVERSITY OF WEST GEORGIA
CARROLLTON GEORGIA

University Press of America, Inc.
Lanham • New York • Oxford

Copyright © 1998
University Press of America,® Inc.
4720 Boston Way
Lanham, Maryland 20706

12 Hid's Copse Rd.
Cummor Hill, Oxford OX2 9JJ

All rights reserved
Printed in the United States of America
British Library Cataloging in Publication Information Available

Library of Congress Cataloging-in-Publication Data

Statham, E. Robert.
The constitution of public philosophy : toward a synthesis of freedom and responsibility in postmodern America / E. Robert Statham, Jr.
p. cm.
Includes bibliographical references and index.
1. Political science—United States—Philosophy. 2. Law—United States—Philosophy. 3. United States—Politics and government. 4. Enlightenment—United States. I. Title.
JA84.U5S72 1998 320.973'01—dc21 98-16032 CIP

ISBN 0-7618-1110-9 (cloth: alk. ppr.)
ISBN 0-7618-1111-7 (pbk: alk. ppr.)

IRVINE SULLIVAN INGRAM LIBRARY
STATE UNIVERSITY OF WEST GEORGIA
CARROLLTON GEORGIA

™ The paper used in this publication meet the minimum requirements of American National Standard for information Sciences—Permanence of Paper for Printed Library Materials, ANSI Z39.48—1984

To my beloved Cherrymar

Irvine Sullivan Ingram Library
DISCARD

Contents

Preface

This work is motivated by a profound sense of intergenerational justice. While the founders of Classical Western civilization and the American regime are no longer alive in body, their words and spirit live on and have left their indelible mark upon future generations, including and significantly my own. This influence of the ideas and thoughts of the past, however, is weakening as individuals in the post-modern West increasingly succumb to the tantalizing seduction of technological sophistication and a relativized and politicized public sphere. I write, therefore, as a seemingly lone voice in the wind of surrounding superfluity as the West, and America specifically, are in evident decline.

My great affection for the brilliance of Western civilization, particularly as it was crystallized in ancient Greece and modified in colonial America, is innate. My love for philosophy and the rule of law are inextricably tied with my sense of what it truly means to be human. That both reason and constitutionalism are endangered causes me pain that transcends my own existence. The great contribution of the West, in both the European and American forms, is that of reason. And, as I write, I see the proliferation of unreason growing almost exponentially.

Post-modern America, my home and place of origin, is in intellectual and moral decay, and I am at a near loss to explain the condition. Could it be that the nation dedicated to the proposition that "all men are created equal" and the assertion that human beings possess certain inalienable rights by nature which government is intended to secure, is now ignorant of its animating goal and purpose? How could such a great and important country lose sight of its core objectives?

America, and the West in general, are in crisis. This crisis is ultimately and fundamentally rooted in unreason. Lost is the vitality of the intrinsic and integral relationship between philosophy and politics, between reason and public life. The crisis is one of public philosophy. A crisis is indeterminate in that either progress or retrogression are potential and open options. It is my sincere hope that a new rebirth of reason will resuscitate Western civilization, and I believe that if this is to take place, it will occur in America.

America must obtain a new consciousness, one which is grounded in the basic tenets of constitutional living as well as the principles and practices of genuine self-government. This renewed consciousness will only take hold through a renewed comprehension of the purposes of the original founding of Classical political philosophy which began with Socrates and of America which began with the framers of constitutionalism, with the new American science of politics. The former resulted in political responsibility whereas the latter produced political freedom. The two are in need of synthesis.

As a young man, growing up in the American West, my parents told me that the United States was suffering from serious moral and intellectual diseases which would ultimately threaten the very Constitution which protected our freedom and unique way of life. They informed me that at some point in the future, the Constitution of the United States would be "hanging by a thread" necessitating a major battle in order to save it from extinction. That time has arrived sooner than I expected, and this work is a preliminary effort toward preserving what might be forever lost. If there is nothing which is worth fighting and ultimately dying for, there is certainly nothing worth living for, and I can think of nothing more worthy of both than the life of contemplative reason which constitutionalism protects and preserves.

The constitution of public philosophy, the theoretical and practical unification of the rule of law with the life of reason—of wisdom and government, is the intention of the following effort. Its importance speaks to the past, present and future. It is, as Abraham Lincoln so properly maintained at Gettysburg, for us, the living, to carry on the great work of those who came before us. We must dedicate ourselves to virtue and justice, to right, to reason, if human existence is to have been, and is to be, genuinely meaningful. It is my earnest hope and intention that politics and reason will obtain the natural coalescence which is their destiny. To this end, the following words have been written.

E. Robert Statham, Jr.
February 8, 1998
Guam, U.S.A.

Chapter 1

Introduction: The Crisis of Public Philosophy

Are we not straying as through an infinite nothing? Do we not feel the breath of empty space? Has it not become colder? Is not night and more night coming on all the while?

Friedrich Nietzsche
The Madman

Western civilization is in crisis. The crisis of Western civilization stems from a denial of truth and a betrayal of the essence of humanity. The West has discarded political philosophy. A civilization which excludes political philosophy must eventually retrogress toward incivility and barbarism as the foundation for higher culture is reason. The role of political philosophy in society, the pursuit and transmission of wisdom by reason, is now all but extinct. The crisis of Western civilization is a crisis of public philosophy, of the role of reason in public affairs.

At a time when constitutional democracy should conceivably be basking in the triumphant light of victory over totalitarianism following two World Wars and a Cold War, Western civilization and American constitutionalism in particular, are in disrepair. Walter Lippmann diagnosed the problem in 1955 when he noted that "there has developed in this century a functional derangement of the relationship between the mass of the people and the government." Lippmann understood that mass opinion has come to dominate government and public policy despite the fact that "a mass cannot govern."[1] This "revolt of the masses" which Jose' Ortega y Gasset so thoroughly described and explained has permeated every facet of our lives, including the intellect:

> a characteristic of our times is the predominance, even in groups traditionally selective, of the mass and the vulgar. Thus, in the intellectual life, which of its essence requires and presupposes qualification, one can note the progressive triumph of the pseudo-intellectual, un-qualified, unqualifiable, and, by their very mental texture, disqualified.[2]

The loss of the qualification and cultivation of the intellect has led to an impoverished condition of human affairs unprecedented in history. We have never been so free externally, and yet so internally enslaved. There is indeed a "Closing of the American mind" and it is the direct result of a pronounced depreciation of contemplation.[3]

Lippmann diagnosed the crisis of public philosophy as the loss of the traditions of civility in the West and traced the dilemma to modern mass ignorance of ideas. He wrote:

> Because ideas have the power to organize human behavior, their efficacy can be radical. They are indeed radical when, as the image of what a man should be, they govern the formation of his character and so imprint a lasting organization on his behavior.[4]

The character forming influence of ideas is extremely weak in our mass age which brought Ortega y Gasset to the following conclusion:

> The average (mass) man finds himself with "ideas" in his head, but lacks the faculty of ideation. He has no conception even of the rare atmosphere in which ideas live. He wishes to have opinions, but is unwilling to accept the conditions and presuppositions that underlied all opinion. Hence, his ideas are in effect nothing more than appetites in words . . . (emphasis added).[5]

Political philosophy is the attempt to replace opinion of the political with knowledge of the political.[6] This endeavor is shunned in post-modernity. Enlightenment rationality has produced human scientific-technological giants who are intellectual and moral dwarfs.[7] Human beings have empowered themselves without engaging the faculty of reason, without obtaining self-mastery. Thinking has become instinctual, passionate, narrowly interested—it has become overwhelmingly pragmatic. Put directly, genuine thought, thought intended to understand, to comprehend, to know, no longer persists. The absence of the attempt to replace political opinion with knowledge of the political has resulted in the predominance of opinion. In the post-modern world, everything is reducible to opinion, therefore, everything is political. We are headed for a second "Stone Age."

Plato, in Book VII of the *Republic*, utilizes the "Allegory of the Cave" to examine the relationship between opinion and knowledge (between politics and political philosophy). The cave is essentially closed to genuine thought but is nevertheless dependent upon it for its well-being. Political philosophy is the ascent from the cave by means of inquiry and the subsequent descent back into to it as an obligation of that inquiry. Without political philosophy, the cave becomes entirely closed, excluding the very possibility of casting the light of reason upon the cave wall shadows, upon opinion.[8] There is an essential relation between political philosophy and natural right, between wisdom and justice which has been either discarded or ignored in our time.[9]

Political science, what was once termed political philosophy, "is suffering from a difficulty that originates in its very nature as a science of man in historical existence." The discipline has turned away from the "search for truth concerning the nature of the various realms of being," and has, therefore, failed in its obligation to cast light upon the shadows, the critical illumination and clarification of the standard of civilization, of nature.[10] Political philosophy discloses what is right by nature and in this way informs convention or society. The dilemma of post-modernity is rooted in the radical separation between nature and humanity, between wisdom and politics which Enlightenment rationality has produced beginning with Machiavelli and extending to our time. The modern age which the Enlightenment ushered in has now become questionable as a result of the neglect of the most important questions, humanly speaking.

In the specific case of the United States, this problematic has arisen in large part as a result of the incomplete nature of the American founding. The American framers developed a new science of politics grounded in the protection of the rights of humanity within the context of written law and the principles of freedom and equality. Their endeavor, and particularly the work of Publius in the *Federalist*, was a remarkable advance in the science of government and politics, one which ought to be preserved and cherished. As sound as the founding was however, it was nevertheless insufficient.

The deficiency of the American founding relates to an incomplete conception of freedom. Freedom consists of two parts: 1) negative freedom (freedom "from") and 2) positive freedom (freedom "to") which are by nature, dialectically associated.[11] The American framers were correct in basing their project upon the understanding that negative freedom from tyranny (the rule of will of the one: tyrant, few: oligarchy, and many: democracy) must be established in order to achieve positive freedom.[12] Their effort was deficient, however, in comprehending the extent and degree to which negative freedom, once instituted, is dependent upon positive freedom for its survival and perpetuation. The two poles of freedom are, to reiterate, dialectically inseparable by nature. Whereas one must be established in practice prior to the other (negative before positive) they are both interdependent (negative then requires positive).

The foundation of negative liberty is a written constitution which incorporates the principles of the separation of powers, checks and balances, federalism, and republicanism. Constitutionalism serves to prevent or limit tyranny by enabling "the government to control the governed," and by then obliging "it to control itself."[13] The foundation of positive liberty is self-government. There are two sources for informing self-government, one religious and the other philosophical (the Judeo-Christian tradition and the tradition of classical political philosophy—Jerusalem and Athens, Faith and Reason).[14] It is these two foundations which are in decline contemporaneously, the result of which is a serious depreciation of self-government.

The American framers separated church and state, conscience from political power, without addressing the intellectual and ethical basis for self-government. They governed themselves but did not produce a philosophic treatise on self-government. The American founding lacked an articulation of a public philosophy of self-government. The framers can be forgiven for not having produced a public philosophy as their needs were unique and historically situated. Additionally, they were Americans and therefore pragmatists—their theory was their practice and their practice their theory. However, self-government does, nevertheless require a standard. That standard can be religious in the particular or local sense, but can only be philosophical in the general or political sense.[15] The foundation for self-government in a free, constitutional order must be political philosophy. Political philosophy is the contemplative pursuit of wisdom which is identical with the discovery of nature, the transcendental standard for justice, which is "trans-historical, trans-social, trans-moral, and trans-religious."[16]

The American, substantially Enlightenment-based constitutional forms secure negative freedom, but are dependent upon political philosophy. Political philosophy ultimately links justice of the soul (individual) with social/political justice by nature via reason, creating the medium by which different and unequal individuals and groups can not only coexist, but live well together. Justice is the end of government whereas knowledge of justice is the interest of political philosophy. The interest in society which has justice as its own interest is political philosophy. Political philosophy is in this way the most important interest in a constitutional order where diverse interests are protected and allowed to freely proliferate. The free proliferation of interests must be guided by that interest which assures that that free proliferation is in the interest of justice. Political philosophy is the role or interest of reason, of justice in public affairs. Political philosophy *is* public philosophy.

The American regime requires, demands the role and interest of political philosophy in order to maintain responsible self-government. Freedom from tyranny cannot exist without freedom to live responsibly and self-sufficiently. Political philosophy instructs citizens regarding the life of self-sufficiency, the life of reason, the life of genuine freedom, the examined life (in the Socratic sense), the best life. Political philosophy teaches free and equal citizens how to pursue the happiness which is their right by nature and which the Constitution protects.[17]

The intent of this research is one of a) locating the decline and crisis of Western civilization and United States constitutionalism in the deficiencies of Enlightenment rationality as applied to the political domain, and the incomplete nature of the American founding, b) examining the essential relationship between constitutional society and political philosophy, and c) articulating how the establishment of a guiding, directing, and ordering role for political philosophy in our time will complete the dialectic of freedom and resolve the crisis in question. The subject of the work is therefore *The Constitution of Public Philosophy*.

How can public philosophy (here defined as the role and interest of reason in society) be constituted in a free, democratic–egalitarian order in which the foundations of political judgment are deemed to be the product or outcome of competing, relative interests (i.e., pluralistically derived and relative)?[18] It is the contention of this research that there is an essential relationship between political philosophy (pursuit of wisdom) and social/political justice. It is also asserted that the discipline of American political science, the core of which is political philosophy, has strayed significantly from its roots by embracing the scientific study of politics and by approaching political phenomena pragmatically.[19] The problematic is evident. The constitution of public philosophy is contingent upon the health, the vitality of political science or philosophy and American political science is not well. For decades there has been collective dissatisfaction within the discipline and the various critiques of political science in the United States have been severe, if not devastating.[20] The constitution of public philosophy can only occur if there is a revitalization of political philosophy within the discipline of American political science.

To emphatically state that American political science must become philosophical is a tall order in a polity in which "the precepts of Descartes are least studied and are best applied."[21] But this is the problem exactly. Western civilization, and America specifically, are in need of the very thing they avoid and even despise. That a proposal is distasteful does not make it any less sound or worthwhile, and in this instance, the opposite is the case. The post-modern West, of which the United States is a key, essential part, is in dire need of the bitter medicine of reason. And the discipline which must swallow the pill and subsequently introduce the same therapy into civil society is American political science.

The primary objective of political philosophy and science has traditionally been the education of citizens toward enlightened citizenship, statesmanship, and education proper. Civic education is the preserve of political science. The discipline has progressively failed in this endeavor and the consequences are devastating as there are nearly two generations of Americans who are poorly equipped to successfully govern themselves.[22] American political science must inculcate in the citizenry public virtue (intellectual and moral), and this it has failed to do. "Walter Lippmann may have been right when he said that the prevalent type of American education, if it continues, is destined to destroy our civilization," and American political science must take responsibility for this condition.[23]

There is an intricate connection between American citizenship, self-government, and the process of becoming fully human. Citizenship in a free, constitutional order is fundamentally a way of life, one which must be guided by a transcendental standard of the qualitatively "best" life. The first political philosopher, Socrates, lived the "examined" life and he was the first and most important example of the best citizen. Socrates was the best citizen because Socrates was most fully human—his life unified philosophy and politics with the former guiding the latter. American political science or philosophy must therefore play a Socratic role in society by educating the citizenry in wisdom and virtue. Socrates ended his *Apology* by appealing to his fellow citizens:

> When my sons are grown up, I would ask you, 0 my friends, to punish them; and I would have you trouble them, as I have troubled you, if they seem to care about riches, or anything, more than about virtue; or if they pretend to be something when they are really nothing—then reprove them, as I have reproved you, for not caring about that for which they ought to care, and thinking that they are something when they are really nothing. And if you do this, I and my sons will have received justice at your hands.[24]

If American political scientists are not the "friends" of Socrates, they betray their own discipline. It is their obligation, it is the heart and soul of their discipline, to educate the citizenry in reason, and therefore self-sufficiency or self-government. The constitution of public philosophy is ultimately rooted in the constitution of American political philosophy.

This work is dedicated to the establishment of a role and interest of political philosophy, of reason in post-modern America. The constitution of public philosophy is the most important and pressing problem of our time. In his "Address at Gettysburg," Abraham Lincoln rededicated the American nation to the "unfinished work," to "the great task remaining before us," of securing "a new birth of freedom" in the United States. President Lincoln presented his remarks in the midst of an American civil war, a struggle which hinged upon "the proposition that all men are created equal."[25] Post-modern America is experiencing a second civil war, rooted in a battle over the verity of this proposition and all principles of truth and wisdom.

Human beings cannot divorce themselves from reason and nature without loosing their essential humanity. This is particularly and acutely the case in a polity like the United States which is dedicated to and perpetuated by such principles. The constitution of public philosophy would rededicate the American nation to the principles which give it meaning. Aristotle begins *The Politics* by stating that "observation tells us that every state is an association, and that every association is formed with a view to some good purpose."[26] He concludes the *Nicomachean Ethics* by explicating exactly what that good purpose is:

> Therefore for man, too, the best and most pleasant life is the life of the intellect, since the intellect is in the fullest sense the man. So this life will also be the happiest.[27]

Philosophy cannot, in the strictest sense, be made popular. However, a populace dedicated to the natural rights of "life, liberty, and the pursuit of happiness," cannot, in the strictest sense, survive and flourish without acknowledging that the security of natural rights must be measured against a transcendental standard of the best life, against what it means to live, to be free, and to be happy—without philosophy. To lay the foundation for the articulation and establishment of this measure and standard is the animating intention of this endeavor.

Chapter 2

The Constitution of the Rule of Law: Justice as the Negation of Tyranny and the Preservation of Liberty

But what is government itself, but the greatest of all reflections on human nature?

James Madison

There can be little doubt that the Constitution developed by the United States framers marked a profound advancement in the science of government and politics. American constitutionalism evolved out of the empirical circumstances of initial British/European tyranny and the eventual societal chaos and governmental disorder of confederalism (the failure of the Articles of Confederation). In fortunate defiance of historical precedent, the Americans found themselves with an opportunity of determining their own destiny by the lights of an unusually large number of individuals with the moral and intellectual training to accomplish the task successfully. The result of their efforts was the production of a form of government which was unsurpassed in its ability to prevent tyranny and procure liberty.

The United States is a liberal country in the sense that it came about through pronounced change by way of a break with certain European traditions.[1] The belief in the basic natural rights of individuals, equality before the law, the separation of Church (religious/philosophical conscience) and State, and the rule of law were all components of the American revolution. Pragmatism, the emphasis on experimental living toward practical progress is not uniquely American, but it does form the basis of the intellectual pre-disposition of most Americans.[2] This being the case, questions arise regarding American traditions and their conservation. The constitutional founding in both thought and practice represents the origin and heart of United States tradition. For this reason it deserves a detailed examination.

I

The American framers, and particularly the authors of the *Federalist,* were greatly, although not entirely influenced by Enlightenment rationality. The Enlightenment (beginning in approximately the 1600's) marked a genuine change in the direction and purpose of political thought. Whereas Classical political philosophy (Platonic/Aristotelian) was fundamentally directed toward the utilization of human reason to obtain comprehensive human (natural and political) understanding, Enlightenment rationality was grounded in the utilization of mind in order to alter existing circumstances for the better.

Greek political philosophy placed primary emphasis upon idealism and the formation of good character in individuals in order to procure social and political justice. This assumed that while untutored human nature is unquestionably passionate and destructive of political ends, it could be cultivated and improved through proper education. The ancients aimed high by giving primacy to political philosophy (the pursuit of wisdom) and maintaining "self-improvement" as the goal of the polis.[3] Following Machiavelli, the emphasis of political thought shifted from idealism to realism. In stead of fixing the goal of a polity upon what a good citizen "ought" to be, efforts were made to make empirical observations regarding the lowest common denominators of human nature in order to arrive at operational generalizations regarding what a typical citizen "is" like. The goal of Enlightenment or modern political thought in this way was lowered so as to obtaining practical political control and efficiency through the development of appropriate institutions.[4] This deviation from the ancients entailed the de-emphasis of the role of political philosophy in the political sphere and highlighted the role of instrumental rationality in securing societal "self-preservation."

An analysis of the *Federalist,* the theoretical explanation of and justification for the Constitution of 1787, provides insight into the extent to which the political ideas of the founding were significantly moored in Enlightenment rationality. At the core of the *Federalist* is a skeptical view of human nature which forms the basis for the creation of the rule of law. James Madison recommended that the very definition of government is contingent upon "the greatest of all reflections on human nature," and proceeded to assert in one of the most notable passages in American political thought that:

> If men were angels, no government would be necessary. If angels were to govern men, neither external nor internal controls on government would be necessary. In framing a government which is to be administered by men over men, the great difficulty lies in this: you must first enable the government to control the governed; and in the next place oblige it to control itself.[5]

By asserting that men are not angels, Madison suggested that realistically, human beings are not ultimately capable of full self-government. The explanation for this concern is found in a skeptical (but not cynical) view of human nature.

Madison and a number of his contemporaries were accomplished students of political philosophy and were particularly well-versed in the writings of the Enlightenment period. One of the thinkers who made a noticeable impression on Madison in particular was David Hume. In utilizing the classical model of the human soul with the tripartite division between the entities of spirit, appetite, and reason paradigmatically, Hume maintained that "the most lively thought is still inferior to the dullest sensation."[6] He claimed that passion rules and is predominant over human reason and subsequently formulated this observation into a general law of human nature:

> It is universally acknowledged that there is a great uniformity among the actions of men, in all nations and ages, and that human nature remains still the same, in its principles and operations. The same motives always produce the same actions: the same events follow from the same causes. Ambition, avarice, self-love, vanity, friendship, generosity, public spirit: these passions, mixed in various degrees, and distributed through society, have been, from the beginning of the world, and still are, the source of all actions and enterprises, which have ever been observed among mankind.[7]

Hume's consideration that passion is by nature stronger in the human sole than reason is one which pervades the logic of James Madison's defense of constitutionalism. Madison contended that human reason is fallible and that its free exercise is grounded in a connection between an individual's opinions and passions, between thought and self-love.[8]

In Madison's view, if individuals are given freedom, they will immediately pursue their own perceived self-interest by forming narrowly interested groups or factions which would militate against both the public good of society as a whole (the aggregate, permanent interests of the community) as well as the rights of other citizens.[9] From his perspective there is a direct relationship between the predominance of human passion over reason and interest group tyranny. Madison considered factions to be the primary problem of freedom, one which he too believed to be a characteristic of human nature:

> The latent causes of faction are thus sown in the nature of man; and we see them everywhere brought to different degrees of activity, according to different circumstances of civil society. A zeal for different opinions concerning religion, concerning government, and many other points, as well of speculation as of practice; an attachment to different leaders ambitiously contending for pre-eminence and power; or to persons of other descriptions whose fortunes have been interesting to the human passions, have, in turn, divided mankind into parties, inflamed them with mutual animosity, and rendered them much more disposed to vex and oppress each other than to co-operate for their common good.[10]

Alexander Hamilton maintained a similar skepticism of human nature and believed that even respectable citizens could be led astray (through honest errors of minds) by preconceived jealousies and fears such as ambition, avarice, personal animosity, and party opposition.[11] The basic problem of government and liberty was, from the perspective of the framers, one of controlling for human unreason.

II

If human beings are, as a general rule, considered to be not fully capable of causing reason to predominate over passion, then the question of central importance regards the creation of external institutional devices to moderate and check the products and effects of passionate human nature. In discussing constitutional checks and balances, James Madison suggested that human beings are partly reasonable and partly unreasonable. The former was for him a virtue and the latter a vice. He insisted that "it is reason, alone, of the public, that ought to control and regulate the government," and that "the passions ought to be controlled and regulated by the government."[12] This equation can be reduced to the argument for the rule of reason via the institutional-governmental moderation of passion. Madisonian skepticism is based upon the belief that while "a dependence on the people is, no doubt, the primary control on the government," human "experience has taught mankind the necessity of auxiliary precautions."[13]

The fundamental principle upon which the early Americans were in agreement was that of "self-government". The practical issue which needed to be addressed was how to create the appropriate institutions to reinforce the principle. The selection of institutions is inextricably linked to the question of human nature which was answered skeptically, but perhaps realistically by the framers. Whereas public virtue is of vital necessity to a polity, it cannot arguably be the sole basis for constitutional self-governance. The relation between human nature and self-government is a complicated one which formed the basis for the American founding. The early American perspective was based upon a mixture of trust in the people to be self-governing and a suspicion that they could not be entirely so. In order for Americans to be virtuous, they had to be free and this was the matter of ultimate concern to the founding generation. Implicitly, however, this also presupposed that Americans would need to be virtuous in order to preserve their liberty.[14] The American constitution of the rule of law was an effort to prevent tyranny and preserve liberty. The need to accomplish this task via external mechanical devices derives from the consideration that the people were quite capable of exhibiting selfish and short-sighted motives which would need to be refined and processed constitutionally.[15] This could be accomplished by positing a general view of human nature and creating institutional structures and mechanisms to anticipate and control for it. James Madison in this way recommended that ambition must be made to counteract ambition" constitutionally so as to 1) protect the people from the government, and 2) protect the people from themselves.[16]

The human experience can to some extent be viewed as a dialectical interaction through time between the polar-opposite forces or conditions of tyranny (rule of will) and anarchy (no rule whatsoever). The European Americans were, from this perspective, largely reacting to the tyranny of their time. Their strongest desire was naturally one of preventing such tyranny and securing natural liberty. Without liberty, any attempt to live well or pursue public virtue would be superfluous. The prevention of tyranny and the preservation of liberty requires the constitution of government.[17] The *Declaration of Independence* makes clear that governments are instituted among men to secure unalienable natural rights.[18] Indeed, the American revolution was fundamentally directed toward the renunciation of tyranny and the eventual adoption of a written constitution which could prevent the rule of will from occurring in any of its various forms. The American desire for and belief in self-government was rooted in a profound experience with and understanding of tyranny. The purpose of government in this way would need to be largely contraventional.

The Classical approach to government and politics was positive. The law would state what was allowed and all else was forbidden. The American, Enlightenment-based approach was predominantly negative. The law would declare what was forbidden and all else would conceivably be allowed. The American development of constitutional government and society was very much inspired by the idea that the purpose of government is to 1) pursue the public good (the good of society as a whole), and 2) protect the basic rights of individuals. The purpose of law would in this way be that of preventing governmental tyranny as well as tyranny between citizens primarily the tyranny of factions). American constitutional justice is not, at the core, positive justice. A detailed explanation of what justice is requires political philosophy in the Classical sense and the new American science of politics was substantially Enlightenment-based.

American constitutionalism developed out of a clear knowledge of and experience with what justice is not. It was a reaction and response to social and political rule of will. Constitutionalism creates a good society by institutionally preventing injustice. The auxiliary precautions which prevent injustice or tyranny are the rule of a higher organic law, the separation of powers, checks and balances, federalism, and the republican principle of representation.[19] Liberty is in this way preserved, but left largely to the people to experience and define. The public good is procured and the basic natural rights of individuals are protected by instrumentally preventing the evils of passionate human nature.

III

The aim of any polity must initially be directed toward self-preservation. Once this goal has been reached, the objective of self-improvement can be sought after. The early Americans were unique in that they were fortunate enough to have had the opportunity of establishing a new nation through reflection (reason) and choice (free of tyranny or force).[20] The spirit which animated the framers was one of securing the blessings of liberty.[21] The American conception of the rule of law was centrally based upon an idea of negative freedom where the government would be limited to the function of maintaining order while protecting life liberty and property from internal and external threats, leaving the individual to live freely, without willful intrusion.[22] The political liberty which the framers intended to secure was not positive or internal, but was the instrumental, practical creation of the conditions of freedom. They focused their efforts upon securing negative liberty as the basic purpose of constitutional forms was to provide freedom from tyranny.[23] The negative liberty which the early Americans desired to secure was rooted in a deep attachment to independence and privacy whereas the characteristics of positive liberty such as capacity, opportunity, and power were fully intended to be placed in the domain of freedom created by the constitution.[24]

There are two main explanations for why the early Americans placed emphasis on the instrumental prevention of tyranny. The first is based upon the conception of property developed by John Locke in his *Second Treatise of Government*. Locke referred to a classically authoritative source in Western civilization, the *Holy Bible,* to recommend that individuals possess certain rights by nature and that natural reason allows them to readily comprehend what those rights are. One of the most basic natural rights is the right to self-preservation. Self-preservation requires freedom from internal or external threats and is in this way inextricably linked to the right to liberty in the negative sense. According to Locke, every individual has a property in his own person which includes the labor of the body, the thoughts of the mind, and any other associated talents.[25] Since the earth is "given to the children of men, given to mankind in common, (Psalm cxv. 16)," Locke asserted that mankind had also been "given reason to make use of it to the best advantage of life and convenience."[26]

> Whatsoever then he removes out of the state that nature has provided and left it in, he has mixed his labor with, and joined to it something that is his own, and thereby makes it his property. It being by him removed from the common state nature has placed it in, it has by his labor something annexed to it that excludes the common right of other men.[27]

The "Labor Theory of Value" which Locke proposed formed an integral part of the American outlook and provided the constitutional foundation for self-preservation. James Madison placed Locke's conception at the core of constitutional theory and practice by emphasizing the principle of equality of opportunity. He understood that pure democracy "can admit of no cure for the mischiefs of faction" and recognized the error in supposing that:

> by reducing (instrumentally) mankind to a perfect equality in their political rights, they would, at the same time, be perfectly equalized and assimilated in their possessions, their opinions, and their passions (emphasis added).[28]

Madison appreciated the relationship between negative liberty and natural differences and inequality between human beings. He therefore held that "the protection of the diversity in the faculties of men, from which the rights or property originate is the first object of government."[29] From Madison's perspective, a basic obligation of government was to reinforce Locke's theory of the natural right to self-preservation. He knew that by protecting individuals in their right to self-preservation equally by law, "different degrees and kinds of property immediately results," and that "the various and unequal distribution of property would be the most common and durable source of factions."[30] For this reason he maintained that "the regulation of various and interfering interests forms the principle task of modern legislation."[31] Constitutional negation of tyranny would in this way include the protection of the diversity of faculties, talents, and associated interests which preserves equality in natural inequality. Individuals would be considered equal before the law in their inequality and diversity. Equality rightly understood is in this way congruent with the standard of nature.

The second objective sought by the American framers was the preservation of liberty of conscience. Here too, the political thought of John Locke provided a source of inspiration. Locke held that having a property in personhood included having a natural right of conscience or reason. Both the *Second Treatise on Government,* and the *Letter on Toleration* inspired Thomas Jefferson's defense of liberty of conscience in the Declaration of Independence.[32] The First Amendment of the U.S. Constitution also forbids laws "respecting an establishment of religion, or prohibiting the free exercise thereof," which derives from the principle of the natural right or liberty of conscience. Constitutional government depends on that right being secured.[33]

Liberty of conscience is in need of institutional protection since the passions and opinions of humanity have a reciprocal influence upon each other which is the primary cause of the oppression and violence of factions.[34] "A zeal for different opinions concerning religion, concerning government, and many other points" has historically led to passionate social and political conflict and has often resulted in one opinion being forced upon others willfully.[35] For this reason, the early Americans sought to distinguish "statecraft" from "soulcraft", Church from State. Taking care of souls is not the role of constitutional government, but protecting souls from external oppression certainly is. In protecting liberty of conscience, constitutionalism promotes the civic ethic of toleration.[36]

The ethic of toleration, far from being based upon atheistic grounds, is actually rooted in the diverse yet sincere religious and philosophical beliefs of the founding generation. Left to live freely in the positive sense as a result of constitutional forms, the early Americans did not share a common religious heritage in terms of sects, and to force such commonalty would have been contrary to the standard of nature. Directly, the natural rights to life, liberty, and happiness articulated in the *Declaration of Independence* cannot be disassociated from the deepest convictions of the heart, mind, and soul. Such matters of conscience are naturally pluralistic and varied.

Liberty of conscience also provides a safe domain for a matter of conscience which is rare in modernity but vitally essential for a good society. The negative liberty preserved by the Constitution protects the natural right of reason. While the American, Enlightenment-based regime did not place contemplative reason as the civic ideal, it did protect such activity from external threats. Just as an individual has the right to worship as he or she sees fit as a matter of conscience, that same individual has the right to reason. The protection of the natural right of reason provides a positive, free sphere for the role of reason in both private as well as public life. This is no small achievement since prior to the institution of the U.S. Constitution, philosophy and political philosophy in particular could only be engaged in as a matter of grace or chance. American constitutionalism aimed short of recommending the rule of philosopher kings as it was and is based upon a skeptical view of human nature and the ability (generally speaking) of human beings of allowing reason to genuinely govern passion. However, the protection of the right of reason leaves open the possibility of political philosophy, of the role of reason in American life, as indirect as this might prove to be.

IV

The genius of American constitutionalism is grounded in the establishment a kind of rule of law which effectively negates tyranny and preserves liberty. The early European Americans were:

> born in a country which had been agitated for centuries by the struggles of faction, and in which all parties had been obliged in their turn to place themselves under the protection of the laws, their political education had been perfected in this rude school; and they were more conversant with the notions of right and the principles of true freedom than the greater part of their European contemporaries.[37]

The framers astutely directed their efforts toward the goal of "self-preservation", an object which is essential to any polity and which forms the foundation for the pursuit of justice. They understood that once tyranny is prevented, the possibility of self-government becomes realizable and meaningful. The forms of constititutionalism secure the public good (justice) and private natural rights (personhood—i.e., labor, conscience, as well as property) and in this way create the conditions of free-living in the positive sense.[38]

It is difficult for post-modern individuals to comprehend the significance of the American advance in the science of politics, perhaps due to the fact that the liberty that the Constitution and its animating principles have preserved is often taken for granted. Political liberty is only secured by way of sacrifice and great exertion.[39] After having experienced well over two centuries of the blessings of liberty, Americans appear to be enslaved to the passions which tend to bring a democratic nation to the point of poverty, servitude, and barbarism.[40] Radical egalitarianism has taken hold of the hearts and minds of contemporary Americans as a result of the two inner vices which are associated with personal and public irresponsibility: selfishness and pride. It would appear that the instrumental negation of tyranny and preservation of liberty by the rule of law are necessary, but insufficient foundations of constitutional justice.

Chapter 3

The Crisis of Constitutionalism: Confronting the Intellectual and Moral Malaise of Liberty Absent Responsibility

There is a deep disorder in our society which comes not from the machinations of our enemies and from the adversities of the human condition but from within ourselves.

Walter Lippmann

The American framers made it perfectly clear that justice is the end of government and civil society.[1] What is also evident is the increasing internal disorder of post-modern American civilization. In apparent disregard of the fact that contemporary Americans experience more freedom than any other people in the history of humanity, there is a growing sense that individuals are denying the responsibility of self-government and engaging in activities which lead to personal and public chaos and destruction.[2] Abraham Lincoln observed that if the United States were to ever fail, it would occur from internal forces:

> At what point then is the approach of danger to be expected? I answer, if it ever reach us, it must spring up amongst us. It cannot come from abroad. If destruction be our lot, we must ourselves be its author and finisher. As a nation of freemen, we must live through all time, or die by suicide.[3]

But what are the potential sources of American internal destruction? Is it possible that a society that had reached the pinnacle of free-living through the institution of the rule of law and adherence to the principles of constitutionalism could ultimately live in denial of both?

I

There are a number of causes for the current social and political turmoil in America, but the source of the problem is both intellectual and moral. America is experiencing a constitutional crisis which derives from the incomplete nature of the original founding.[4] This constitutional crisis is not so much grounded in deficiencies of the Constitution or its animating principles (although some fine tuning is arguably required), but is related to the philosophical aspects of free-living. America is experiencing a crisis of public philosophy.[5]

America is a country which is very much bound together by a common method of thought and action. Americans are, for better and for worse, pragmatists.[6] Their "social condition deters them from speculative studies" or contemplative philosophy and their value of equality causes each individual to judge everything for himself or herself resulting in a "taste for the tangible and the real, and a contempt for tradition and forms."[7] Americans tend to favor knowledge which is practically useful and this propensity fits well with the social condition of equality and a political economy based upon competition, production, and merit. American pragmatism, however, has also resulted in a profound neglect of the philosophical foundations of constitutionalism and it is this lack of proper care that has produced the crisis of public philosophy.

The pragmatism of the American framers and Enlightenment rationality fit together nicely sense both outlooks emphasize methods or techniques of thought. Human thought can ultimately be divided into two distinct but inseparable domains. The first, which is the most basic, is "rationality", mind directed toward knowledge of practical efficiency or skill. Rationality, generally speaking, is the intellectual attempt to acquire knowledge of "know how", such as how to make fire, find food and shelter, prevent disease, defend oneself in combat, find water, etc.. The intellectual aspects of athletics, for example, are rooted in rationality. A boxer must strategically anticipate how the opponent will attack in order to put up a defense, and must alternatively develop techniques for attacking the opponent in order to engage an adequate offense. The kind of thinking required in boxing as in other sports is rationality.

The other kind of thinking, which is of a higher order, is reason. Reason is mind directed toward comprehensive understanding or wisdom. Reason is strictly a human endeavor as lower animals do not possess such a faculty. The ground of human reason is initial recognition of mystery, or a sense of wonder regarding the things which matter most to human beings. The raising of questions falling into the category "What Is?" (such as What is happiness?, What is love?, What is justice?) can be referred to as the activity of reasoning. It is the genuinely deliberative component of human thought.[8] Whereas the best examples of individuals who have mastered rationality are athletes and lawyers, Socrates provides the most poignant example of an individual who had mastered reason.

The American founding was very much inspired by both rational and reasonable objectives. In fact, the ideals of freedom from tyranny and the right to self-government are rooted in human reason. Thomas Jefferson eloquently stated "We hold these truths to be self-evident" in *The Declaration of Independence* indicating that the principles of equality and natural right were the products of pure, unassisted human reason. Moreover, the framers sought to remedy the weaknesses of pure democracy while maintaining democratic forms by constituting democracy in such a way as to regulate it. In this regard they remained true to the political thought of Aristotle which understood pure democracy to be a perverted form of rule, and constitutionalism to be just.[9]

The *Federalist,* as the primary theoretical explanation for the Constitution, is perceptibly a product of Enlightenment rationality. Whereas justice is viewed to be the end of government in the work, a philosophical inquiry into the principles of a just constitutional society is not undertaken.[10] By making a general skeptical observation regarding human nature which is based upon passion predominating over reason, the framers were able to devise a constitutional framework which could quasi-automatically anticipate passionate human behavior in its variety of expressions and regulate it. The objective was one of predicting and controlling for the kinds of human behavior which would threaten the regime and the liberty it was intended to preserve. Constitutionalism is a technological apparatus of human design intended to regulate human nature.

It would, however, be erroneous to presuppose that the authors of the *Federalist* considered all human beings to be equally incapable of causing reason to predominate over the passions. Indeed, the following passage from Paper #55 states:

> As there is a degree of depravity in mankind which requires a certain degree of circumspection and distrust, so there are other qualities in human nature which justify a certain portion of esteem and confidence. Republican government presupposes the existence of these qualities in a higher degree than any other form. Were the pictures which have been drawn by the political jealousy of some among us faithful likenesses of the human character, the inference would be, that there is not sufficient virtue among men for self-government; and that nothing less than the chains of despotism can restrain them from destroying and devouring one another.[11]

According to James Madison, the aim of every political constitution ought to be one of obtaining rulers who are most wise and virtuous to pursue the common good of society.[12] He did, nevertheless, qualify this contention by recommending that effectual precautions be taken for keeping such representatives virtuous.[13] And yet, are the mechanical devices the framers invented sufficient guards of public virtue?

The *Federalist* and the Constitution it explains and defends are authentic works of pragmatic realism. Constitutionalism is a form of government based upon preventing the lower, more base characteristics of human nature from predominating in society while simultaneously recognizing that higher characteristics of human nature could then not only exist, but flourish in the activity of self-government. It provides the conditions for the realization of positive liberty and political justice by preserving negative liberty and preventing tyranny, or injustice. In this respect, American constitutionalism represents a marked advance in the science of politics.

There is, however, cause to consider the possibility that the work of the framers is sound, but incomplete. Liberty is comprised of two essential components, one negative and the other positive. Negative liberty can be defined as freedom "from" whereas positive liberty can be defined as freedom "to".[14] The American framers utilized Enlightenment rationality and a rich understanding of politics and government to devise constitutional mechanisms which preserve the former. The early Americans, as a general rule, understood well how to utilize their newly created domain of positive liberty. They lived in accordance with the principles of positive liberty, they lived responsibly, they understood and accepted the public philosophy of self-government.

No people can live freely without living virtuously. Public virtue is of particular necessity in circumstances where the institutions of government are limited and the domain of self-government is expanded. And yet, the principles of public virtue were not written into the Constitution (this is altogether impossible), and the public philosophy of self-government was never explicitly stated or written in the form of a treatise.[15] The work that the framers left unfinished is the provision of the conditions of the second component of positive liberty which must accompany the first (negative liberty). Genuine freedom cannot exist without responsibility, and the principles of responsible free-living must be found in the public philosophy. The Constitution rationally preserves the conditions of negative liberty by preventing tyranny, while the public philosophy provides the intellectual/moral foundations for positive liberty, for self-government. The public philosophy articulates the role of reason in American life.

The contemporary crisis of constitutionalism is derivative of the neglect of the public philosophy of self-government which Walter Lippman believed created a great social vacuum:

> In our time the institutions built upon the foundations of the public philosophy still stand. But they are used by a public who are not being taught, and no longer adhere to, the philosophy. Increasingly, the people are alienated from the inner principles of their institutions. The question is whether and how this alienation can be overcome, and the rupture of the traditions of civility repaired.[16]

Constitutionalism frees individuals from tyranny, but only education in and adherence to the public philosophy can assist them in living well in their freedom. Eric Fromm considered that modern humanity, "freed from the bonds of pre-individualistic society" has not "gained freedom in the positive sense."[17] He estimated that "the majority of men have not yet acquired the maturity to be independent, rational, to be objective," and suggested that without qualitative development of human reason, individuals would ironically attempt to "escape from freedom":

> The problem of freedom is not only a quantitative one, but a qualitative one; that we not only have to preserve and increase

> the traditional freedom, but that we have to gain a new kind of freedom, one which enables us to realize our own individual self, to have faith in this self and in life.[18]

Fromm ultimately perceived that the crisis of our time is not simply the product of excessive individualism, but is the result of individuals experiencing freedom in profound intellectual and moral immaturity.

To assume that individuals can live freely without extensive training in the public philosophy of self-government can only lead to social and political conditions of disorder and decay. Where the institutions of government are intentionally limited so as to create a free sphere, the responsibility for government is at once transferred to individuals and their respective families and communities. Making individuals free from external rule without providing them with the necessary education in how to successfully engage in self-government has produced what Ortega y Gasset referred to as "the revolt of the masses". The "mass" man is not isolated in a specific socioeconomic class. He or she is the average individual who "pronounces judgment upon anything which is in disagreement with his common-places" and who "crushes beneath him anything that is excellent, individual, qualified, and select."[19] A substantial portion of the educational preparation for responsible free-living is based upon the development of the intellectual faculties which limit passion and produce human excellence and nobility.

Alexis de Tocqueville's assessment of the American anti-intellectual disposition parallels that of Ortega y Gasset. Whereas the latter held that the "mass" man "accustoms himself not to appeal from his own to any authority outside him," the former described Americans as possessing an intellectual character which conformed to their social conditions of equality:

> The practice of Americans leads their minds to other habits, to fixing the standard of their judgment in themselves alone . . . they readily conclude that everything in the world may be explained, and that nothing in it transcends the limits of the

> understanding. Thus they fall to denying what they cannot comprehend; which leaves them but little faith for whatever is extraordinary and an almost insurmountable distaste for whatever is supernatural.[20]

As is evident from the above mentioned observations, the "great vacuum" created by the contemporary neglect of public philosophy is related to a void of reason. Once the "mass" man finds that he/ she has been voluntarily been offered freedom from external constraint, he/she immediately asserts the right "not to be reasonable" and his/her opinions become mere expressions of passions or emotions. To have ideas requires an individual to have reasons for having them.[21] This demands an appeal to the authority of reason which transcends the subjective self and the passions of opinion the authors of the *Federalist* were so wary of. The "mass" individual lives in ignorance of such a standard absent education in the public philosophy.

When reason no longer forms the basis for society, then the mind "becomes the instrument of appetite, desire, and passion" and "the instinctive impulses determine the end of all activities" where "mind is but . . . the instrument by which those impulses seek their satisfactions."[22] Put differently, a mind untutored in the public philosophy will undoubtedly be enslaved to the passions it rationally serves to fulfill. This is what James Madison meant when he claimed that there is a connection between the opinions and the passions in which "the former will be objects to which the latter will attach themselves."[23] The individual untrained in the public philosophy is incapable of self-government.

Paradoxically, the same individual who is internally enslaved to his/her passions, refuses to acknowledge external authority or standards of any kind (including reason). The empowerment of the masses without cultivating within them a proper understanding of and respect for the public philosophy results in the leveling of all standards in the interest of mediocrity. Constitutionalism proper is a standard which requires limits, indirect methods, courtesy, restrictions, and formality.[24] Thus, even the standard of the rule of law is denigrated by individuals who are not properly trained in the principles of responsible free-living. Constitutionalism cannot exist without an accompanying public philosophy, without the authoritative standard of reason.

The crisis of constitutionalism is not altogether surprising. Constitutional democracy is that most formidable attempt of allowing the people to rule, albeit indirectly. The rule of the people does not come without costs, significant ones. The price of limiting the institutions of government and providing for widespread self-government is education in the principles of self-government. This sort of education is difficult to inculcate into the masses as their tastes and desires are naturally removed from refining intellectual and moral forms. Tocqueville Understood the problem well:

> Is it your object to refine the habits, embellish the manners, and cultivate the arts, to promote the love of poetry, beauty, and glory? . . . If you believe such to be the principle object of society, avoid the government of democracy, for it will not lead you with certainty to the goal. But if you hold it expedient to divert the moral and intellectual activity of man to the production of comfort and the promotion of general well-being; if a clear understanding be more profitable to man than genius; . . . if, instead of living in the midst of a brilliant society, you are contented to have prosperity around you . . . if such is your desire, then equalize the conditions of men and establish democratic institutions.[25]

To the extent that the people in a constitutional democracy can be educated in the public philosophy, that education must necessarily be of a rudimentary, limiting nature. At the most basic level, self-government requires the internal capacity and willingness to live within responsible limits and the public philosophy which articulates such limits is desperately needed since the virtues of self-sacrifice and limited self-government are "already fleeting far away from us" and the "time is fast approaching when freedom, public peace, and social order itself will not be able to exist without such education."[26]

II

The United States Constitution secures the conditions of freedom from tyranny but is insufficient for providing the requisite principles for positive liberty. Constitutional government secures the possibility of self-government by negating threats to it. However, it cannot, and was not intended to govern in the active, positive sense.[27] The two components of liberty (negative and positive) form a dialectic. The Constitution secures negative liberty by limiting or negating the deleterious characteristics of human nature. Constitutional mechanisms instrumentally function to prevent passion from dominating public life by regulating interfering interests.[28] The positive component of liberty is in this way placed in a free private sphere. The responsibility for self-government resides with the people. Self-government, if it is to be taken seriously, means *"self-government"*. The people are responsible for governing themselves in constitutional society, without external institutional interference. What the law governs is limited. The limits of the law are found in the negation of tyranny. Positive free-living by definition means living to a great degree without external coercion. The missing element of the constitutional equation is the public philosophy of positive self-government.

In *Federalist* #51, James Madison attempts to explain how the Constitution would guard the rights of individuals. His argument clearly reflects the instrumental concept of justice as negation:

> It is of great importance in a republic not only to guard the society against the oppression of its rulers, but to guard one part of the society against the injustice of the other part. Different interests necessarily exist in different classes of citizens. If a

> majority be united by a common interest, the rights of the minority will be insecure. There are but two methods of providing against this evil: the one by creating a will in the community independent of the majority—that is, of the society itself; the other by comprehending in the society so many separate descriptions of citizens as will render an unjust combination of a majority of the whole very improbable, if not impracticable.[29]

Madison maintained that the first method of providing against interest group tyranny would be insufficient as an independent force or will is found in governments based upon hereditary rule or self-appointed authority.[30] He chose the second method, the extension of the federal republic so as to "break society into so many parts, interests and classes of citizens, that the rights of individuals, *or* of the minority, will be in little danger from interested combinations of the majority."[31] Intriguingly, Madison selected the second method since it is pragmatic. The extension of territory is a practical, instrumental adjustment which serves to diversify interests and therefore passions, sufficiently to prevent majoritarian tyranny. For the majority to govern, it would then have to do so on the basis of deliberation and compromise.

Of critical importance is Madison's dismissal of the possibility of creating an independent will in society. His Enlightenment based rationality precluded further development of this most essential alternative. While an extension of the territory diversifies interests, it does not in any way intimate the positive principles upon which those interests might be deliberated upon. An extended republic is a remarkable contraventional device as history has demonstrated, but an independent will in society is of even greater importance. Self-government cannot occur automatically, and the "trial and error" or "sink or swim" methods of learning are untenable in the instance of self-government.

The framers, as a general rule, attempted to create a constitutional mechanism that could regulate and control passion. The passions would in this way be "controlled and regulated by the government."[32]

The extension of territory in the republic, for example, is an external device which regulates passions by presupposing their existence and proliferation and instrumentally preventing them from becoming tyrannical. In *Federalist #10,* Madison maintains that factions cannot be controlled by either destroying liberty, or by "giving every citizen the same opinions, the same passions, and the same interests."[33] Instead, he recommends that government serve as a regulator, an arbiter between the various and interfering interests.[34] This instrumental approach to self-government is a well-conceived, but partial remedy.

The extended republic which Madison believed would mechanistically prevent the kind of majoritarian tyranny which is characteristic of small republics has, absent the public philosophy of positive self-government, created a number of misconceptions regarding constitutional government which has led to a rampant proliferation of group-based competition in the political sphere. In extending the republic, interests are indeed diversified and the groups that hold these interests proliferate. True, majoritarian tyranny is precluded, but so is national consensus regarding the rule of law and its animating principles. Aristotle maintained that every society is "an association formed with a view to the Good."[35] By extending the territory, majoritarian tyranny is effectively negated, but the core principles of the regime are blurred and abrogated.

Absent an independent will or force in a constitutional society, the Madisonian mechanism of preventing tyranny becomes the complete end to which individuals and groups are directed. In many respects, Theodore Lowi was accurate in arguing that the Constitution of 1787 and its forms have been pragmatically dislocated by pluralistic interest-group liberalism.[36] Harvey Mansfield diagnosed the problem in suggesting that:

> The trouble with modern constitutionalism is that civil liberties and man-made constitutional forms are made subordinate to the natural end that comprises life, liberty, and the pursuit of happiness. *They are a **means** to that end, not united with it; the*

> *form is not united with the end*, as in Aristotle's constitutionalism (emphasis added).[37]

The consequence of "the constriction of rationality to instrumentality (power and control)" is the exclusion of the "possibility of speaking rationally (or reasonably) about the ends or purposes of power."[38] In its social application, if instrumental rationality dominates public life, mind becomes a means by which the people attempt to satisfy their conceived desires, and "politics in its modern sense of power struggle is the logical result."[39]

The difficulty to be confronted is serious. If the end of 'constitutional government is the prevention of tyranny, equality before the law, and genuine self-government, then the government cannot be primarily responsible for controlling and regulating the passions of the people, but only secondarily so. External control and regulation of passions is a topical, stop-gap remedy which does not go to the source of the problem. The extension of territory (as well as the other auxiliary precautions) secures negative liberty. But this alone simply over-extends the republic. Negative liberty taken as an end results in the politicization of society and a depreciation of the possibility of positive self-government. Where no independent will exists to moderate the passions, outside the institutions of government and the law, everything becomes political. Jacques Ellul understood this modern problematic:

> Man in his entirety is being judged today in relation to political affairs, which are invested with ultimate value. In our judgment everything has become political and political affairs are the ultimate guidepost. Beyond them there is nothing. And political affairs can be judged only by political considerations. . . . And man's participation in the collective *via political channels* are the ultimate value symbols and criteria of our time, substituted for the religious symbols and criteria of the past. . . . As soon as modern man involves himself in politics he *is animated by a passion without measure. In our day political conflict has*

> *definitely become the decisive and ultimate form of conflict* (emphasis added).[40]

The absence of an independent will creates a void which is invariably replaced with passionate, positive, political, group-based activity, or selfish apathy. The security of negative liberty, by itself, has unleashed the explosive politicization of our time. Our age is one of fanaticism. Individuals, once free of external threats, are compelled to join a cause, any cause, and if necessary, to sacrifice their lives for their beliefs.[41] Those who do not join a cause, indignantly refuse social responsibility of any kind.

III

The present crisis of constitutionalism derives from the attempt to give negative liberty to the people, the many, while presupposing that their passions, as a general rule, predominate over their reason. Constitutional contraventional government only counters passion with passion, "ambition vs. ambition" without addressing the root of the problem.[42]

What post-modern America is confronted with is a circumstance in which constitutional forms are considered to be sufficient safeguards of liberty when in point of fact they are insufficient. The inadequacies are found in near total politicization of American life (even the structure of the family/household and relations between men and women have become exceedingly controversial), and concomitant institutional over-load. Constitutional structures have, as a result of the failure of self-government, increasingly been relied upon to accomplish the tasks of positive liberty. Limited government can only occur when the people take upon themselves the responsibility of positive self-government. And yet, the people have no guide to the principles of self-government. Freedom and equality are not effectively connected to the end of self-government producing the crisis in question.

When the conditions of freedom from tyranny are secured without accompanying authoritative directives, anarchy eventually encroaches upon the free sphere requiring positive, external intervention. Eric Fromm described the current situation as one in which people who have not progressed from negative freedom to positive freedom would become overwhelmed by their emotions of "aloneness, fear, and bewilderment." Individuals who are not internally self-governing ultimately, in Fromm's view, resort to symbiosis, a circumstance in which they sadistically and masochistically escape freedom by attempting to dominate each other in order to avoid the integrity of the "self" and make others completely dependent upon them.[43] The passion which predominates over a non-self-governing individual is, ironically enough, will. Nietzsche's concept of "the will to power" is both explanatory of and applicable to the human condition of isolated negative liberty.[44]

> What determines the nature of 'truth'? The nature of I which asserts 'I am the truth'. . . . The great need, the 'one thing needful', was to overcome the nihilistic devaluation of life and man which had followed the destruction of the metaphysical world (the 'death of God'). And when Nietzsche came to understand fear as the feeling of absence of power, he was left with a single motivating principle for all human actions: the will to power.[45]

Human nobility and excellence is by definition associated with great personal effort and exertion leading to freedom being linked with responsibility and right connected with a sense of duty. Alternatively, barbarism tends toward disassociation and "the pullulation of tiny groups, separate from and hostile to one another."[46] The average individual, upon being made free without being instructed in the principles of positive freedom, turns to the barbaric endeavor of attempting to enforce his/her will upon others. The non-self-governing individual is a slave to his/her will to power who ultimately desires to tyrannize (defined as "rule of will") others.

The attempt to constitutionally and externally regulate passionate human beings creates a new form of anarchic tyranny.

When James Madison contended that the public good is disregarded in the conflicts of rival parties, he perceptively addressed the fundamental problem of a free constitutional society. However, in neglecting the necessity of an independent force or will in society, he misunderstood the full equation of freedom. The crisis of American constitutionalism is not so much legal or institutional as it is cultural. Ortega y Gasset discussed the essential aspects of culture as follows:

> What I affirm is that there is no culture where there are no standards to which our fellowmen can have recourse. There is no culture where there are no principles of legality to which to appeal. *There is no culture where there is no acceptance of certain final intellectual positions to which a dispute may be referred* (emphasis added).[47]

The regulation of factions must be both external (legal) and internal (philosophical). Madison was correct in considering the destruction of liberty an undesirable remedy for hypergroupism. Yet, his suspicion of "giving to every citizen the same opinions, the same passions, and the same interests," was only partly accurate.[48] Indeed, human reason is fallible, and human beings are self-interested. But they must, as Ortega y Gasset recommends, possess certain fixed opinions, passions, and interests which bind them together.

The bond of free constitutional society must be the independent force or will in society. That independent will is the public philosophy of positive self-government. The "preservation of the spirit and form of popular government" can only be derived from a dialectical integration of contraventional constitutional forms based upon a skeptical view of human nature and informed principles of self-government based upon the philosophic nurture of passionate human nature. Passion requires force, but passion demands reason. Constitutionalism must of necessity be mated with political philosophy.

Chapter 4

The 'Self-Refuting' American Science of Politics: Pragmatism, Democratic Pluralism, and the Depreciation of Public Philosophy

> *The new political science denies in a way that there is a public reason: government may be a broker, if a broker possessing "the monopoly of violence," but it surely is not the public reason. . . . By teaching the equality of all values, by denying that there are things which are intrinsically high and others which are intrinsically low as well as by denying that there is an essential difference between men and brutes, it unwittingly contributes to the victory of the gutter.*
>
> Leo Strauss

It is perhaps an irony of ironies that the science which is responsible for cultivating good government and political justice in the United States has often contributed to their decay. The causes of this tragedy are rooted in a combination of an almost singular pursuit and perpetuation of pluralist democracy and the nearly unconscious utilization of pragmatic rationality as a means to this democratic end.[1]

The purpose of this chapter is not to exhaustively indict American political science for an over-emphasis upon methodology and a neglect of genuine political inquiry since this has already occurred.[2] What is remarkable, if not astonishing, is the extent to which the discipline has ignored the sound critiques of its tendencies and proclivities. The intent is therefore one of articulating the specific manner in which American political science has in some instances expanded and in others distorted or perverted the weaknesses of the original founding project of constitutional democracy.

I

To a significant degree, the crisis of Western civilization is a crisis of constitutionalism.[3] And the crisis of constitutionalism derives largely from a depreciation of genuine contemplative political inquiry in favor of pragmatic-methodological rationality in the service of pluralist (group-based) democratic political action. Directly, the classical goal of political philosophy, which is the intellectual pursuit of wisdom or final knowledge regarding politics, has been supplanted by the attempt to conform the study of politics to the criteria of positivist natural science.[4] And the placing of method over contemplation, which requires the distinction between facts and values is, in and of itself, not "value-free". The motive behind methodistic social science is largely one of perpetuating a kind of democracy (radical/egalitarian/pluralist) which is antithetical to the constitutional (or qualified) democracy envisioned and instituted by the American framers.[5]

Whereas the basic weakness of the American founding was the development of institutions which would anticipate and regulate the pernicious negative effects of passionate human nature short of fully addressing the need for a coherent positive-constructive public philosophy, modern American political science has tended to misinterpret the framers original project by assuming that the United States Constitution is a regulating device for groups (factions) competing for power at the exclusion of the animating principles of constitutionalism.[6] Justice from this approach is not transcendental but is grounded in group competition, and government is viewed as a mere broker between them while power becomes the exclusive goal of democratic politics. Whereas the political theory of the *Federalist*, for example, is primarily concerned with the regulation of groups in order to prevent tyranny (particularly that of the majority) so as to provide for genuine self-government guided by the principles of freedom and equality rightly understood, American academic political science has been based upon a view of democracy which directly conflicts with the framers intentions. Groupism was viewed by the framers as *the* problem to be solved.[7] American political scientists have tended to make this problem the goal of the polity.[8]

Americans are, as a general rule and by their nature, pragmatists. This Alexis de Tocqueville immediately discerned in his work *Democracy in America* as he noted the extent to which this pragmatic tendency of mind and action caused Americans to be "more addicted to practical than to theoretical science."[9] Tocqueville, a French aristocrat, well understood the different categories of mind (theoretical, theoretical/practical, and practical application) and he observed that in the United States "'hardly anyone devotes himself to the essentially theoretical and abstract portion of human knowledge."[10] American political science generally serves as a mirror which accurately reflects American anti-intellectualism. The following passage from Tocqueville's perceptive work is instructive on this point:

> Men who live in democratic communities not only seldom indulge in meditation, but they naturally entertain very little esteem for it. A democratic state of society and democratic institutions

> keep the greater part of men in constant activity; and the habits of mind that are suited to an active life are not always suited to a contemplative one. The man of action is frequently obliged to content himself with the best he can get because he would never accomplish his purpose if he chose to carry every detail to perfection. He has occasion perpetually to rely on ideas that he has not had leisure to search to the bottom; for he is much more frequently aided by the seasonableness of an idea than by its strict accuracy; and in the long run he risks less in making use of some false principles than in spending his time in establishing all of his principles on the basis of truth.[11]

Tocqueville understood the great resistance of democratic peoples in general to engage in or respect contemplative political philosophy. The American addiction to practical science has been pronounced and the shape it has taken is an emphasis upon methods of thought directed toward the reinforcement of democratic beliefs.[12]

When theoretical relevance is subordinated to method, science is no longer directed toward the search for truth regarding political phenomena. Eric Voegelin, for example, pointed out that:

> if method is made the criterion of science, then the meaning of science as a truthful account of the structure of reality, as the theoretical orientation of man in his world, and as the great instrument for man's understanding of his own position in the universe is lost.[13]

Voegelin's point is of considerable importance as indeed, American political science has been mired in disciplinary atomization for decades as a direct result of the impoverishment of contemplative political philosophy within the field.[14] Method (falling under the categorical question "How To?") requires substantive guidance which can only be provided by contemplation toward wisdom or knowledge (falling under the categorical question "What Is?"). In the United States, method takes primacy and, consequently,

American political scientists have, to quote from Theodore Lowi's scathing indictment of the discipline, "become what they once studied".[15]

Not having the desire to pursue general transcendental knowledge regarding politics and more specifically constitutional democracy, American political scientists have tended to assume that the purpose of their endeavor should simply be the cultivation, reinforcement, and perpetuation of pluralist-egalitarian democracy. A sober analysis of the American founding of "constitutional" democracy would have prevented this proclivity, but such was never intended. When political philosophy ceases to be the guide for political inquiry, inquiry is pushed to the side while methods of thought are utilized for the purpose of advocacy. When "the *episteme* is ruined, men do not stop talking about politics; but they now must express themselves in the mode of *doxa*," or opinion.[16] The expression of opinion on behalf of pluralist-egalitarian democracy is ideologically driven as in democratic times individuals presume that the solution to democratic problems is more democracy. American political scientists have politicized the discipline to the extent that, according to George Carey:

> their "science" is both a shield and a tool: a shield to mask their ideology, to give their work the veneer of objectivity; a tool to validate or lend credence to, whenever possible, the tenets of their ideology.[17]

Where the pursuit of transcendental knowledge is discarded, there can only be opinion. Contemplative political philosophy is the attempt to replace opinions regarding politics with knowledge, it is the intellectual ascent from opinion to knowledge.[18] Where thought is utilized to reinforce opinion regarding pluralist-egalitarian democracy, nothing can be thought of or for, except that opinion. In this way, political thought becomes the reinforcement, as opposed to the questioning of, opinion. This pragmatic approach to political science is anti-inquirical. Thinking that is utilized to actively reinforce democratic opinion is inherently political. This is the root cause of the politicization of American political science. Where knowledge is not the goal of thought, political interest (opinion) is the natural replacement goal.[19]

II

The pragmatic tendencies of American society suggest that to know is to do and to do is to know.[20] American political and social scientists have therefore tended to assume that the solution of political problems comes from direct participation in politics, through vigorous political action. Yet, while genuine self-government requires participation by individuals, the principle upon which such participation originally rested was that of limited government.[21] The idea that the institutions of government were to be held to certain limits was integral to the principle of freedom (the negative prevention of tyranny, of rule of will). Once free as a result of the institution of the rule of law (a written constitution), individuals, families, communities, and the nation were to proceed with the endeavor of freely governing themselves. Where American political science has become pragmatically diverted from these principles is in assuming that positive government must be the preserve of the State (particularly the Federal Government) and that the purpose of political action is rooted in interest-group liberalism.[22]

Statism and interest-group liberalism (previously referred to as pluralist-egalitarian democracy) are in direct conflict, as has been stated, with the principles of constitutionalism. The rule of law is intended to prevent tyranny of any kind, and in a democracy the most pernicious kind of tyranny is group-based factionalism. For this reason James Madison held that the primary object of government would of necessity be "the regulation of various and interfering interests."[23] American political scientists have, however, replaced the concept of limited government, which makes a clear distinction between an *extensive* private sphere of self-government and a *limited* public sphere of institutional government, with the idea that the purpose of politics is maximum political participation requiring the extension of institutional government (i.e., legislation and regulation) from the top-down to nearly every aspect of daily life.[24] This approach assumes that the answers to human problems can somehow be resolved through the process of group-based participation in politics whereas the framers, and the authors of the *Federalist* in particular, considered the need for constitutional government to be derivative of a human nature which requires restraint.

E.E. Schattschneider, in his work *The Semisovereign People*, suggested that politics can be defined in such a way that "the nature of political organization depends on the conflicts exploited in the political system."[25] His view of democracy in the United States deserves to be quoted at length in as much as it accurately reflects the intellectual disposition of many American political scientists:

> Democracy is a competitive political system in which competing leaders and organizations define the alternatives of public policy in such a way that the public can participate in the decision-making process. . . . The exploitation of this situation by responsible political leaders and organizations is the essence of democracy; the socialization of conflict is the essential democratic process.[26]

Again, it is clear that the preceding view of politics is grounded in a misinterpretation of constitutional democracy driven by a pronounced value of pluralist-egalitarian democracy. More importantly, this view assumes that the basis of American society and democratic societies generally is disagreement and competition. Inherent in this view is a denial of a substantive transcendental interest of society, a public good. To assert that the basis of society is group exploitation of political conflict is to tantamount to the reduction of the political (which is of necessity by nature dependent upon a common good) to the subpolitical.[27] Put differently, the essence of American society cannot possibly be found in interest-group liberalism and the augmentation of the State. To quote one of the most important observations of Aristotle, "every state is an association, and every association is formed with a view to some good purpose."[28]

III

The pragmatic American science of politics is "self-refuting" in that 1) it places interest-group pluralism as the main goal of the American polity which is actually the most fundamental of problems to be regulated constitutionally by the rule of law, and 2) elevates instrumental rationality (thought which is strategic in terms of narrow group interests) above contemplative reason. A civilized society requires a general purpose or good which serves as an animating principle. Without a public good, there is no "reason" for the existence of a comprehensive social whole. American academic political science, in promoting pluralism (the sub-political) and the augmentation of the State, has increased hyper-groupism and the concomitant hyper-extension of the sphere of public conflict which requires governmental/institutional intervention. This serves to depreciate the rule of law as well as responsible self-government. The propensity to emphasize instrumental rationality has occurred at the expense of the public role of political philosophy (what is classically referred to as political philosophy), the role of reason in society.

To a certain extent, the pragmatic characteristics of American political and social science reduce the political sphere to a quasi state of nature where groups compete for control and power producing an over-load on the constitutional framework. James Madison asserted that the "latent causes of faction are . . . sown in the nature of man."[29] Whereas constitutional government is intended to regulate the passions which lead to factionalism, American political science has tended to fuel factionalism by emphasizing the need for political group-based action and participation. The problem lies not in participation proper or the formation of groups as both are natural and indeed essential to a well-functioning free society, but is rooted in the belief that political action must of necessity be directed toward the State or the public sphere without limitation as a societal end, in and of itself. "Limited government is free government, in which a people is free because it governs itself freely."[30] The elevation of democratic pluralism to the position of a goal for the American polity results in an underlying equation of justice with State might (might makes right). The thought of the *Federalist* suggests that groups pursue their own partial interests against the protection of the basic natural rights of individuals and the public good (the principled interest of society as a whole) since groups by nature are only concerned with their own narrow interests.[31] Madison observed that "a zeal for different opinions concerning religion, concerning government, and many other points" divides individuals into separate divergent factions and he noted that:

> The friend of popular governments never finds himself much alarmed for their character and fate, as when he *contemplates* their propensity to this dangerous vice. He will not fail, therefore, to set a due value on any plan which, without violating the *principles* to which he is attached, provides a proper cure for it (emphasis added).[32]

The American pragmatic science of politics characteristically shuns philosophy in the classical sense. The utilization of methods of thinking raises the obvious question of what exactly the methods are intended to accomplish and which ends they are meant to serve. "Methodology is mind engaged in the legitimation of its own political activity," it is "the political action which thought takes on the route (hodos) to being (logos)."[33] In other words, methodology is inextricably associated with some purpose. Unfortunately, in the case of American political science, the purpose has been antithetical to the Constitution and its animating principles.

IV

The basic intention of the framers was that of 1) developing a general theory of human nature in an effort to ascertain certain common denominators of political behavior, and 2) creating the appropriate institutional devices to anticipate that nature in practice. Human nature was the standard upon which the political institution of a written constitution was based. Constitutionalism was specifically designed to instrumentally preclude the perpetual fluctuation between tyranny and anarchy through time, in this way maintaining the public good and protecting the basic rights of individuals by regulating groups. And yet, over two centuries later, constitutional democracy is in decay and it would appear that we are no longer fully or genuinely protected by the rule of law.[34]

Constitutionalism is insufficient without a transcendental foundation. Without a principled justification, the rule of law becomes meaningless and impotent.[35] While the political thought of the *Federalist* provides a partial remedy for the pernicious aspects of human nature and particularly factionalism, it does not put forth a positive public philosophy for the regime that it recommends. American political science has not provided relief in this regard, but has simply persisted in emphasizing pragmatic rationality directed toward the sphere of political action in the form of advocating pluralist democracy and Statism. Where the *Federalist* takes one step (however incomplete) forward, American political science has taken two steps back.

The need for a public philosophy requires taking the words "public" and "philosophy" literally. The founding project is deficient insofar as it failed to put forth an argument for and in behalf of the elusive "independent force" James Madison discussed in *Federalist* #51. In relying predominantly upon instrumental rationality to address the basic problems of free democratic living, Madison developed the institutional mechanism of an extended territory. He understood that since it is of great importance "to guard one part of society against the injustice of the other part," and an extension of the territory of the republic effectively secures the rights of citizens by creating "a multiplicity of sects."[36] To cite Madison's own words:

> Whilst all authority in it (the United States) will be derived from and dependent on the society, the society will be broken into so many parts, interests and classes of citizens, that the rights of individuals, or the minority, will be in little danger from interested combinations of the majority (emphasis added).[37]

The extended republic concept has certainly worked as majoritarian tyranny has often been prevented and the rights of individuals and minorities have been largely (with some exceptions) protected.

Nevertheless, is there not the possibility of an over-extension of the territory of the republic which could conceivably create excessive divisions and disunity? And, in addition, can an extension of territory and a multiplicity of sects, in and of itself, produce social and political justice? Preventing tyranny and anarchy institutionally (externally) is one matter. Promoting unity on the basis of the principled interest of society as a whole (the Public Good) is another. Madison was cognizant of two methods of preventing majoritarian tyranny, but he selected one (extension of territory) over the other, the creation of "a will in the community independent of the society."[38] He believed that the creation of this independent force would be at best "a precarious security" since "a power independent of society may as well espouse the unjust views of the major, as the rightful interests of the minor party, and may possibly be turned against both parties."[39] In other words, Madison's skeptical view of human nature made him suspicious of the very possibility of creating an independent force in society.

Taking the terms "public" and "philosophy" literally results in the understanding that public philosophy is the role of wisdom or reason in public or society. The role of reason in society is the classical definition of political philosophy and political philosophy, by its very nature, is the detached, objective, *independent* quest for wisdom or final knowledge regarding politics. Madison, and the authors of the *Federalist* in general, were skeptical of the possibility of political philosophy in the classical sense because they were skeptical of human nature. This is why the creation of an independent force was considered to be impractical. Consider the following passage written by Madison in *Federalist* #55:

> In all very numerous assemblies, of whatever character composed, passion never fails to wrest the sceptre from reason. Had every Athenian citizen been a Socrates, every Athenian assembly would still have been a mob.[40]

While this is undoubtedly a general statement regarding human nature in terms of social psychology, it nevertheless points toward the genuine skepticism of Madison concerning even the possibility of the existence of individuals who possess the requisite abilities for self-restraint and deliberation.

The skeptical view of human nature found in the *Federalist* is based upon the belief that the creation of a body of individuals who would neither succumb to narrow, parochial advocacy, nor become entrenched in their own self interest is next to impossible. While demonstrating the desire for the constitution of good government by a people based upon reflection and choice, Alexander Hamilton nonetheless asserted that:

> so numerous indeed and so powerful are the causes which serve to give a false bias to judgment, that we, upon many occasions, see *wise and good men* on the wrong as well as on the right side of questions of the first magnitude to society (emphasis added).[41]

Madison considered that the goal of every constitution should first be to obtain rulers who possess most wisdom to discern, and most virtue to pursue the common good in society."[42] However, this desire apparently conflicts with his belief that the reason government is instituted is that "the passions of men will not conform to the dictates of reason and justice, without constraint."[43] The skeptical view of human nature found in the *Federalist*, which is largely a result of the influence of the thought of David Hume and the Scottish Enlightenment, impedes the development of a public philosophy (a role for political philosophers in constitutional society) as an independent force of public reason or wisdom.[44] Where as a general rule, passion is viewed to predominate over reason, reason cannot be expected to prevail in the one, the few, or the many. It would appear that the roots of the "self-refuting" American science of politics can be found, at least in part, in the skeptical view of human nature held by the framers. As far as they went, they remained on safe "preventive" ground. They constituted a regime which presupposed that "ambition must be made to counteract ambition" in order to secure the rights of individuals and pursue the public good. But the consideration that men, as a general rule, are not "angels" and that the institution of government must be largely based upon this assertion places constitutional government in the sole position as regulator of the passions of human beings.[45]

External mechanical devices alone, however, cannot reasonably be assumed to be sufficient regulators of human passions. And the Constitution, the supreme law of the land, is meaningless without an accompanying positive justification. In other words, free constitutional government cannot even be considered practicable without the possibility of human excellence through self-government which requires reason in the best of circumstances to predominate over passion. Institutional (external) regulation of human beings alone contradicts this concept of genuine self-government. If passion rules over reason without exception, self-government is simply not possible. Freedom must ultimately come from within. And for this to occur, the possibility of the creation of a number of individuals in society who can and will, through proper training, pursue political wisdom as a way of life and who will in this way cause reason to predominate over the passions must be real. The number who can actually master this task might be limited, but the example must of necessity proliferate throughout a free, self-governing society so that the citizenry, while reaching this goal in various degrees, maintains this pursuit as an ultimate example of human excellence.

V

The crisis of constitutionalism is a crisis of public philosophy, and the crisis of public philosophy is derivative of the crisis of political philosophy in the classical sense. These relations are essential as the law must be grounded in a transcendental standard if it is to be lasting and meaningful. Law, or the Constitution, in an of itself, is insufficient to procure justice. The law must have an animating purpose (Artistotle's contention) which transcends interest group based partiality and the predominance of passion over reason which is most often expressed through mere convention or positive State action. The transcendental standard of the rule of law can only be ascertained by political philosophy (the contemplative movement from "opinion" to "knowledge"). This derives from the necessary relation between natural reason and political right or justice. The transcendental standard for the rule of law is natural right and the foundation of natural right is reason.[46] Constitutionalism is given meaning by political philosophy as the justification of the rule of law is, and must of necessity be, philosophical.[47]

The modern problem of the relation between politics and philosophy, the crisis of public philosophy, is a problem "which even very good scholars sometimes fail to solve properly," including to a certain extent, the authors of the *Federalist*.[48] There must be, as Leo Strauss observed, an "essential connection between the *eidos*, the form, the character of a city, and the end to which the city is dedicated."[49] Strauss understood that "every political society derives its character from a specific public or political morality, from what it regards as publicly defensible."[50] The lack of continuity between the character of constitutionalism and the end to which it is dedicated is derivative of the impoverished role of political science or philosophy in consistently articulating the connection. It is worthwhile to cite Mansfield again to substantiate this point:

> The trouble with modern constitutionalism is that civil liberties and man-made constitutional forms are made subordinate to the natural end that comprises life, liberty, and the pursuit of happiness. They are means to that end, not united with it; the form is not united with the end, as in Aristotle's constitutionalism."[51]

The discontinuity between the forms of constitutionalism and the principled natural end or ideal which they are intended to secure derives from the problematic nature of modern Western political science proper. The science of politics is "suffering from a difficulty that originates in its very nature as a science of man in historical existence.[52] Eric Voegelin maintained that human society "is illuminated through an elaborate symbolism . . . from rite, through myth, to theory" and "this symbolism illuminates it with meaning."[53] But most importantly:

> the symbols express the experience that man is fully man by virtue of his participation in the *whole which transcends* his particular existence (emphasis added).[54]

At the core of this whole which *transcends* humanity is, according to Voegelin, the *corpus mysticum* or *immanent Logos* of society which can be translated to mean the Public Good.[55] The Public Good is the animating body of principles which give meaning to a society and classically (in Plato and Aristotle for example) the polis or society mirrored the cosmos so that social and political order was predicated upon natural existence and the standard of nature.[56]

Whereas a healthy society "will interpret its order as part of the transcendent order of being" an unhealthy one would conceivably understand itself in terms of itself exclusively.[57] Beginning with Machiavelli and followed by Thomas Hobbes, the emphasis for societal interpretation shifted from a transcendent principle to human nature so that a purpose beyond human existence was effectively denied.[58] Taking a similar approach, David Hume (who significantly influenced the framers of American constitutionalism) defined liberty as "a power of acting or not acting, according to the determinations of the will."[59] In following Hume's emphasis upon human nature, Madison, Hamilton, and their associates devised a constitutionalism which was specifically oriented toward the limitation of will in the form of law. A written constitution prevents injustice (tyranny/anarchy) by creating a sphere of private freedom, thereby producing a domain for self-government.[60] This approach is based upon a general psychology of human nature which presupposes that passion (the strongest expression of which is by nature "will") predominates over reason. A parallel observation would conclude that institutions should predominate over ideas, and law over the articulation of the ideal, or Public Good of society. The framers presupposed, out of radical skepticism regarding the possibility of transcendental reason, that political philosophy (an independent force) was impracticable, if not impossible. And yet, without the illuminating force of reason or wisdom in a free society, all action is reduced to opinion (doxa) within the human non-transcendent realm of passion in defiance and contra nature. A society devoid of political philosophy (the independent force of reason) can only interpret itself in terms of itself which results in total politicization. Absent a philosophic interest in society (which by definition moves from opinion to knowledge and from action to deliberation) to quote from Hobbes' *Leviathan*, "nothing can be unjust. The notions of right and wrong, justice and injustice have no place."[61] Constitutionalism, or the rule of law divorced from transcendental reason, returns to Hobbes state of nature. The most basic human expression of will in the state of nature is in Hobbes' view "a general inclination of all mankind, a perpetual and restless *desire* (a passion) *of power after power*, that ceaseth only in death (emphasis added)."[62]

The only force which can counteract the passion for power after power is a formidable consolidation of power which is precisely why Hobbes prescribed the authoritative rule of a Leviathan. Without a common power to hold the citizenry in awe, anarchy prevails. This is all the result of severing the forms of constitutionalism from their principled transcendental end. By studying the generic nature of man solely in terms of human passions, the problem is created of "constructing an order of society out of isolated individuals who are not oriented toward a common purpose but only motivated by their individual passions."[63] The American science of politics tends to refute itself by not providing the transcendental force and standard which points toward the Public Good or *immanent Logos* of the regime (via political philosophy)—public philosophy. The rule of law is in this way reduced to a matter of power, as opposed to justice. The foundation of society becomes narrowly interested will as opposed to right reason.

That human nature can be generalized to be passionate and willful is a proposition which is difficult to deny. And, that a written constitution which incorporates the instruments of the separation of powers, checks and balances, republican representation, and federalism tends to effectively anticipate the negative aspects of human nature and counter them is even less controversial. Yet, once freedom is instrumentally obtained through such external constraints and restraints, questions remain. On what basis does a free individual live his life and how can that individual govern himself/herself in freedom? What are the moral and intellectual foundations of free-living?[64]

Disregard for the transcendental principles which animate society and the activity which illuminates them (political philosophy) along with the institutional creation of a sphere of freedom impervious to the law inevitably declines into permissive egalitarianism where what is secured is not conscience or reason, but the individual with his urges.[65] Permissive egalitarian democracy protects the unrestrained pursuit of the realization of the passions, and where the passions predominate (as by nature they presumably do), individuals engage in a seemingly infinite variety of sensual, pleasing behaviors, a quasi-animal condition where the emotions and instincts dictate action, the most pernicious and pronounced of which is what Nietzsche termed the "will to power." Constitutionalism, which is predicated upon a negative interpretation of human nature exclusively, proceeds at the ultimate expense of both law and reason. Constitutionalism must have a transcendental justification or the sole reason for existence becomes existence alone. Neglect of the transcendentality of existence relegates humanity to hedonistic pleasure-seeking which ultimately is not particularly innocuous.

Carl Schmitt, (the German Legal Scholar most often known for his association with the Nazi regime in WWII Germany as the "Crown Jurist") in response to what he perceived to be the repugnant effects of modern permissive egalitarianism, developed a reactionary concept of the political where individuals could not avoid the seriousness of human existence and where they would ultimately be forced to decide, fight, and even die for a cause.[66] While Schmitt desired to superimpose his concept of the political upon modernity, he did not address the question of what is right and therefore worth fighting and dying for.[67] The political, as divorced from reason, is animated by nothing other than hedonistic passion.

The founder of modern liberalism, Thomas Hobbes, in the words of Eric Voegelin:

> could not interpret the nature of man from the vantage point of the maximum of differentiation through the experiences of transcendence so that passion, and especially the fundamental passion, *superbia*, could be discerned as the permanently present danger of the fall from true nature; but he had, on the contrary,

> to interpret the life of passion as the nature of man so that the phenomena of spiritual life appeared as the extremes of *superbia*.[68]

Even though the framers of American constitutionalism established their science in terms of self-government and limited government, the absence of a clearly defined role for public philosophy (independent of the institutions of government proper) which would consistently give meaning to the regime has produced the two extremes of *superbia*. The crisis of constitutionalism, which is a crisis of public philosophy, and which has occurred through neglect of the need for an independent role of reason or wisdom in society, has produced two human types—1) apathetic, free-loading, pleasure-seekers who perpetually and instinctually entertain themselves by "having fun", "making contracts", and "going places", and 2) power seekers who make human existence a life or death struggle for power and control as a way of existence.[69] These two human types are often indistinguishable since what drives them is ultimately what they "will". Constitutionalism absent reason refutes itself by perpetuating the two evils which have been the demise of human civilization from the beginning—selfishness and pride. The attempt to frame constitutional society strictly on the plane of humanity (contra the transcendental standard of nature which is understood via reason) is inhumane.

VI

The original controversy between the Federalists and the Anti-Federalists points toward a polarization in American political thought and science which persists to the present, one which must be transcended if the polity is to flourish in the future. One the one hand, the Federalists, and particularly Madison and Hamilton, were fearful of the instability of republican governments based upon the classical model. Such regimes required the government to maintain public virtue.[70] The Federalists relied upon mechanisms which would balance competing interests through the institutions of government in a commercial, competitive republic, thereby relegating public virtue to patriotism, conviction, and self-restraint.[71] The Anti-Federalist position tends to be tied to the traditions of civic republicanism where citizens find their sense of identity and unity in the experiences of political practice.[72] The civic republican tradition does not sharply differentiate between the public and private spheres since cooperation beginning at the level of the community is the prerequisite for social and political cohesion.

In the case of the former, justice is secured by the prevention of injustice through the creation of realistic institutions based upon a sober assessment of human nature. In the latter case, justice is secured through social participation and experience, in an of itself, a view which ultimately rests upon an optimistic consideration of human nature. The weakness of the Federalist position is the assumption that groups of individuals competing within the framework of the constitution without a public philosophy which articulates the basic points upon which all citizens agree is self-sufficient. The limitation of the Anti-Federalist view is the belief that free individuals can govern themselves without external constraints and simply on the basis of political practice.

The issue of contention between Federalism and Anti-Federalism relates to the tension that exists between qualified democracy which is regulated and moderated by constitutional mechanisms (the most prominent of which is an extended republic) and participatory or unqualified democracy where, to quote James Madison, "a small number of citizens . . . assemble and administer the government in person."[73] In the first instance, there is a sharp distinction between the public (government) sphere and the private sphere (individual, community, and society). The public sphere is limited by law while the private sphere is the domain of self-government. In the case of Anti-federalism and unqualified democracy, the public sphere and the private sphere are inseparable and the law applies to both.

What is absent in this tension between the Federalist and Anti-Federalist positions is a comprehensive principled public philosophy which unites the strengths of the two while excluding the weaknesses. Put differently, Federalism requires the social cohesion upon which small republics are based and Anti-Federalism demands external regulation in order to prevent the tyranny and anarchy that invariably pervades pure democracies. In light of the fact that American constitutionalism is fundamentally based upon Federalist forms, it is necessary to revitalize the concept of the Public Good within the framework of human rights, not by reverting to democratization, but by developing the prospects for political philosophy (the role of reason) at every level of society. American constitutionalism requires the interest of political philosophy so that the rights of individuals and minorities might be protected while the Public Good (justice of society as a whole) is secured.[74] Political philosophy links, by way of reason, the forms of constitutionalism with the principled ends to which they are directed. Political philosophy, the philosophical science of the political, breaths life and meaning into constitutionalism. Political philosophy is public philosophy.

Chapter 5

Public Philosophy and the Indirect Rule of Philosopher Kings

Until philosophers are kings, or the kings and princes of this world have the spirit and power of philosophy, and political greatness and wisdom meet in one, and those commoner natures who pursue either to the exclusion of the other are compelled to stand aside, cities will never have rest from their evils,—no, nor the human race, as I believe,—and then only will this our State have a possibility of life and behold the light of day.

Socrates
Plato's *Republic*

Perhaps one of the most misunderstood and disregarded concepts of classical Western political philosophy is the idea put forth in Plato's *Republic* that the best social and political ordering requires the rule of philosopher kings. That such a regime is improbable, due to the fact that philosophers do not by nature desire political power and the people by nature do not desire that philosophers possess such power, is often taken to mean that its conceptualization and implementation is merely a matter of fantasy, not to be taken seriously. Indeed, the primary founder of modernity, Machiavelli, looked at principalities and republics ruled by the wise cynically and his outlook predominates in our time.[1]

However unwilling the current generation is to acknowledge the practicability of philosophic rule as an ideal, it is altogether possible that the deficiency is actually our own. Ours is an egalitarian/pluralistic age in which human distinctions are viewed skeptically unless they pertain to feats of the body or technical skill. This democratic view precludes comprehension of immaterial objects such as ideas, and in this way displaces the world of reason which is predicated upon the contemplation of forms. And yet, it is arguably the task of contemplating forms which we find to be most difficult and unnerving presently. Consensus regarding even the most basic matters of public policy (family governance and affairs, abortion, euthanasia, juvenile crime, etc.) now appears elusive. Paradoxically, at a time when constitutional democracy and its accompanying principles of natural right, freedom, and equality should be celebrated at the close of the Cold War, the concept of right is commonly viewed relativistically, freedom is being replaced by individual and social irresponsibility, and equality is misunderstood to mean equality of factual result. The disease of post-modernity is perceptibly one of unreason. The cure, not surprisingly, appears to the inflicted to be most distasteful. What is lacking if not missing in our time is, nonetheless, the role of reason (which is political philosophy), in private and public life. The rule of philosopher kings (albeit indirect) must now, more than ever, be taken seriously.

I

Since the end of the Middle Ages philosophy in the classical sense of the term has steadily declined in social and political importance.[2] Today, "political philosophy is in a state of decay and perhaps of putrefaction, if it has not vanished altogether."[3] The poor condition of political philosophy (the contemplative quest for transcendental (i.e., non-relativistic/non-subjective knowledge regarding the political) is directly associated with the depreciation of public philosophy in the United States. To reiterate, public philosophy is the role of reason in the public or political sphere, it *is* political philosophy.

In order to clarify this point it is instructive to refer to the argument of Plato's *Republic*. In Book VII, Socrates puts forth the well known "allegory of the cave" in which the cave represents society, the prisoners represent the citizenry, and those who make the ascent from darkness to light are the philosophers. The philosophers question the shadows on the cave wall, unlike their fellow citizens, and in so doing, come to the realization that these images are merely appearances of reality. The philosophic understanding of the partial, incomplete nature of the shadows follows sincere intellectual inquiry. Upon engaging in inquiry by way of questioning, the philosophers comprehend the cave for what it is in reality. And, upon obtaining such knowledge, it is incumbent upon them to return.[4] Indeed, the most important citizens are the philosophers as they are both conscientious and informed. The descent back into the cave is as important as the initial ascent. Whereas the ascent marks the movement from opinion to knowledge, the descent marks the meeting of knowledge with opinion. Political philosophy is a dialectical, intellectually cogitative activity which gives meaning and light to the cave. Without political philosophy, the cave is closed, it is comprised of opinion only. And, a cave or society which is based upon opinion only cannot be just. Justice must be grounded in truth or reality which opinion only reflects in part or partially.

The cave (society) and political philosophy (reason) must necessarily exist as an integration. The subject matter and ultimate concern of political philosophy is the well-being of the cave and the well-being of the cave is contingent upon political philosophy.

Closed caves or societies exhibit all of the symptoms of injustice which invariably derive from human ignorance. Open caves or societies demonstrate the effects of justice which derive from human wisdom. For example, it is quite possible to make a distinction between Pol Pot's "killing fields" in Cambodia and deliberative democracy in the United States. This comparison alone is sufficient to point out the difference between justice and injustice, knowledge and ignorance. Political philosophy is non-existent in the former case, while it is the basis of the latter.

The animating question of Plato's *Republic* is "What is Justice?"[5] The fact that what guides the work is a question indicates its philosophical nature. What is even more striking is the answer which the dialogue offers in response to the question. The *Republic* provides a solution to the question of the qualitatively best social, moral, and political ordering of humanity, one which is obtained through the process of political philosophy. There is then a direct relation between political philosophy and its goal, between inquiry and knowledge of justice. What is most difficult for us in our time to comprehend and to take seriously, if not literally, is not simply that justice is possible, but that it is entirely dependent upon political philosophy. There is an undeniable relationship between justice and reason. Since the current widespread belief is that reason is impossible (due to our acceptance of the proposition that principles and concerns are subjective values and ultimately therefore, relative), justice is inconceivable as well.[6] It is this crisis of political philosophy which has affected the role reason plays in society resulting in genuine doubt regarding the possibility of justice. And yet, the doubtful nature of justice, which is contingent upon political philosophy for its articulation and protection, is the cause of the crisis of public philosophy. Absent political philosophy, society cannot approach justice. There is no such thing as justice without reason. A society devoid of political philosophy is rooted in unreason. A society without the illuminating and moderating role of political philosophy exists without reasonable justification, without public philosophy.

II

The political philosopher Leo Strauss considered that the orientation of modernity and post-modernity, which places primary value on the active life and particularly political action, was misguided. Strauss, in responding to his contemporary Alexander Kojeve regarding the prospects for the twenty-first century, feared the development of a universal and homogenous global state in which reason would be non-existent and which would ultimately lead to a condition of war. Strauss understood that there is an intricate natural connection between reason and humanity. Unlimited technological progress without the guidance of reason (political philosophy) leads to the ultimate human destruction of humanity.[7] In direct opposition to the predominant forces in contemporary American political science which tend to jointly promote global democratization and the creation of a world state, Strauss wondered whether:

> perhaps it is not war nor work but *thinking* that constitutes the humanity of man. Perhaps it is not recognition (which for many men lose in its power to satisfy what it gains in universality) but *wisdom* that is the end of man (emphasis added).[8]

Strauss comprehended the extent to which the most important cause to be taken up for the sake of humanity in our time is that of political philosophy.

Plato's *Republic* is fundamentally based upon the idea that reason is a life ordering, directing, and governing principle.[9] Indeed, the argument of the *Republic* hinges upon Strauss' assertion that "the good order of the soul is philosophizing," and "only by philosophizing can man's soul become well-ordered."[10] The question "What is Justice?" which the work is intended to answer, is inextricably related to the activity of contemplation. What appears on the surface to be the most impractical of endeavors, contemplative reflection, is ultimately the most practical in that without it, life becomes disorderly and meaningless. But if this is the case, what is the direct practical relationship between reason and justice? How is it that philosophizing leads to the well-ordering of the human soul? And, what is the relationship, if there is one, between philosophy, a well-ordered soul, and justice of a society? In what sense is thinking practically efficacious?

Whereas the modern approach toward politics has been rooted in method and the instrumental development of external institutional arrangements based upon a static negative view of human nature (what humanity "is"), the classical approach was based upon the deliberative formation of character (what humanity "ought" to be). Classical political philosophy placed emphasis upon the inner person, upon the soul. The soul is tri-part consisting of reason, spirit, and appetite. The latter two are emotions or passions while the former is intellectually based. By nature, our emotions are predominant.[11] And yet, the classical approach took this as the starting point whereas the modern approach takes this as the ending point. The primary objective of classical political philosophy is that of ordering the soul well. For this to occur, reason must of necessity be trained to moderate spirit and passion. When spirit and/or passion predominate, the soul is unbalanced and enslaved. The classics, therefore, had a rather remarkable understanding of slavery which was based not upon external bondage and forced servitude, but upon internal subjugation due to the absence or weakness of the regulating effects of reason. An enslaved individual is one who simply does not cause reason to balance the soul in such a way that each part does its own appropriate work. The ordering of the soul through the cultivation of reason, through philosophic education, is then the focus of classical political philosophy:

> But in reality justice was such as we were describing, being concerned however, not with the outward man, but with the inward, which is the true self and concernment of man: for the just man does not permit the several elements within him to interfere with one another, or any of them to do the work of the

> others,—he sets in order his own inner life, and is his own master and his own law, and at peace with himself.[12]

This classical approach, which is based upon the formation of character, takes as a given that human beings by nature have passions. All human beings feel anger, sadness, happiness, and frustration for example, and human beings all have desires based upon hunger, sex, honor, love, power, money, and so on. If these emotions are not regulated, they in varying degrees dominate a person. Fortunately, human beings also possess the faculty of reason. This part of the soul, however, requires training in order to function well. The cultivation of reason requires the individual to think through his/her passions so as to moderate them. Reason, as a life ordering, directing, and governing principle, is essential for living well. It is one thing to be alive, and quite another to live well. The *Republic* assumes that one of the most important human concerns beyond existence regards the possibility of living a good life. This concern for living well is in this way directly related to the question of justice and the well-being of the soul. To order one's soul by way of reason produces inner harmony and a harmonious soul is a just soul. Justice of the soul is required in order to live well and justice can only occur in accordance with the principle of reason.[13]

The classical focus upon character formation places the concept of "self-government" at the heart of the philosophical quest for political justice. Indeed, justice is first of all a matter of self-governance. Justice of the soul requires reason to moderate the passions producing freedom since a soul which is dominated by the passions is enslaved. Justice requires the cultivation of reason via philosophic education. The education of character in terms of reason is the foundation of classical political philosophy. Self-government is the intent of character formation, and the formation of character in terms of reason is the fundamental goal of political philosophy. In this way, political philosophy fulfills the ideal of self-government which is the animating goal of a constitutional order.

It is the inter-related nature of political philosophy and self-government that points toward the core of the crisis of American constitutionalism and public philosophy. The forms of American constitutionalism, freedom and equality, are procured by the creation of institutional mechanisms based upon a sober reflection of human nature which assumes that human beings are such that passion rules or predominates over reason. This is why a constitution is necessary in the first place. By preventing the passions from predominating through the institutionalization of the separation of powers, checks and balances, federalism, and republican representation (i.e., the rule of law by written constitution) the *possibility* of freedom and equality in a private sphere is created in opposition to interpersonal and governmental tyranny and anarchy. American Enlightenment-based constitutionalism, in being based upon a skeptical view of human nature, effectively prevents passion from ruling externally, by law. And yet, the only way genuine self-government can occur freely and equally in a private sphere is if individuals are capable of actually governing themselves internally. Whereas the forms of constitutionalism protect the possibility of self-government, they do not provide the necessary instruction in self-improvement. In a sense, American Enlightenment-based constitutionalism is paradoxical. It attempts to create a private sphere of self-government while presupposing that individuals are in actuality incapable of governing themselves. The paradox is only apparent however since indeed, as a general rule, human beings are quite incapable of self-governance: that is, without sufficient and appropriate training. The deficiency of the founding project is rooted in the over-reliance upon a negative conception of human nature and negative liberty. A complete constitution requires not only a negative pole, but a positive one as well. The forms of freedom and equality must be connected with their end which is constitutional justice based upon the ideal of genuine self-government.[14] American Enlightenment-based constitutionalism is in need of the positive role of classical political philosophy. In as much as classical political philosophy aims primarily at the formation of character (upon the cultivation of reason as a life ordering, directing, and governing principle in terms of the regulation of the inner person), it provides the missing component of a complete constitution. The combination of external negative law based upon what human beings by nature are (the United States Constitutional framework) with internal positive law based upon what human beings ought to be (the role of philosophic education in terms of reasoned self-government—public philosophy) completes the dialectic of constitutionalism.

III

In what sense can the combination of Enlightenment-based constitutional forms with the end of self-government by way of philosophic education in reason be said to produce justice in the American polity? This question points toward the relationship between justice of the individual and justice of society as a whole which is emphasized in classical political philosophy and de-emphasized in modernity.

Presently, there is considerable concern regarding the pernicious effects of radical individualism on the one hand where individuals place themselves and their own self-interest above the law and society, and the ever increasing augmentation of the State on the other. Whenever individuals either cannot or will not govern themselves, something or someone else must. Excessive individualism and Statism are actually symptoms of a general decay of both individual self-government and the responsible limited role of the State. When individuals fail to govern themselves, the State over-extends itself. When individuals succumb to their own egoistic passions there is a depreciation of reason and inner imbalance. Once this imbalance begins to emerge, it invariably affects others. For example, if an individual becomes addicted to an illegal drug, it is rare that the effects of the addiction are self-contained. Often such addictions affect family members and citizens of a community in terms of domestic turbulence, crime, etc. Ultimately, the fact that the addicted individual is incapable of self-government results in the necessity of external rule and this is not either quantitatively or qualitatively cost-free. A deficiency of self-government at some point tends to lead toward the growth of the State and/or external governmental institutions, and this is what is progressively occurring in our time.

The argument of Plato's *Republic* is instructive in this regard since from the perspective of classical political philosophy, justice of the soul is justice of society writ large. Self-government beginning at the level of the individual is essential to the well-being of society. Whereas Enlightenment-based constitutional forms focus upon protecting minorities (and particularly individuals) from majoritarian tyranny, the very possibility of individuals living-well in society requires that once free, citizens successfully govern themselves to a large extent absent external coercion. More important yet is the necessary and unavoidable connection between internal self-government at the level of the individual and the order of civil society. To the extent that individuals govern themselves, the necessity of external governmental regulation is decreased so that a perfectly well-ordered society would be one in which individuals are virtually free of external governmental institutions. This anarchistic ideal has tended to thrive in the United States in terms of "rugged individualism" and "libertarianism" due to the close association between local self-government ideals and the goals of constitutionalism.[15]

Clearly the framers were on target in considering that the possibility of creating a free society absent external constraint in the form of law is not possible humanly speaking. And yet, the goal of responsible self-government is vital to the successful development of freedom and equality within the framework of limited government they constructed. Self-government requires positive internal directives which cannot by definition be provided for by constitutional law. In a constitutional regime, the law forbids what is socially unacceptable and individuals are left to freely and responsibly (i.e., reasonably) govern the rest. In contradistinction to classical societies in which the law was prescriptive and all-pervasive, modern individuals are left to decide for themselves absent legal restraint (meaning to deliberately and contemplatively live in freedom). This of course raises the question of how individuals can live "well" in their constitutionally procured freedom. The answer hinges on the ability of individuals to cultivate reason (in varying degrees) so as to internally regulate the passions. It is true that constitutionalism is, in the first instance, based upon the presupposition that individuals are such that their passions predominate over their reason. But it is even more veritable that the well-being of a constitutional order is dependent upon the ability of human beings to internally cause reason to govern the passions.

Individual self-government in terms of the ordering principle of reason leads to justice of the soul which collectively results in social justice. Freedom requires responsible self-government and responsible self-government is contingent upon the existence of freedom.[16] Where individuals responsibly govern themselves via reason, they do their own work. Each individual citizen is a part of a larger whole and each different part has an appropriate function. When each part successfully carries out its function, the whole is just. What is true of the parts of society is indeed true of the whole, and what is true of the whole is true of the constituent parts. The purpose of constitutional society is freedom and equality in terms of self-government. Each citizen fulfills this purpose by governing himself/herself freely and equally before the law in accordance with the principle of reason.[17]

IV

Having established that there is an essential relationship between justice of the soul and political justice writ large, the question of how the principle of reason, which is the basis for justice, can be cultivated and communicated arises. The very nature of the subject cuts against the grain of the common sentiments of our time since reason is a concept which does not comfortably conform to the prejudices of radical egalitarian democracy and relativism.

The principle of reason, which is the foundation of political philosophy, is hierarchical since its standard is nature, and nature is hierarchical. The goal of political philosophy is knowledge of justice, or what is right by nature.[18] To acquire this knowledge political philosophy must attempt to understand nature by reason, a natural human faculty. And an understanding of nature, even at a rudimentary level, discloses the systemic, and essentially differentiated characteristics of physical and biological reality. Reason reflects the distinction between human and natural phenomena and it also brings to light natural distinctions or essential differences between human beings. Of course, the most important distinction reason clarifies regarding human beings is the extent to which different individuals utilize the faculty of reason well or poorly. The faculty of reason makes distinctions between individuals who live reasonably and those who do not. But even this distinction, since it by nature differentiates, tends to conflict with the common love of equality which predominates in our time. Here it is possible to see the connection between radical egalitarianism and relativism as Americans find it very difficult to declare one way of life to be qualitatively better or worse than another—to the extent that ways of life are viewed in terms of style.[19]

Alexis de Tocqueville understood the great conflict that exists between the contemplation of forms (reason) and democracy in America to be rooted in the emotional affection for equality. He noted the connection between reason and inequality which democratic peoples disdain:

> But for equality their passion is ardent, insatiable, incessant, invincible; they call for equality in freedom; and if they cannot obtain that, they still call for equality in slavery. They will

> endure poverty, servitude, barbarism, but they will not endure aristocracy.[20]

Bertrand Russell found that of all the countries he visited throughout his lifetime, America was the most disagreeable. Russell, an aristocrat by birth and a philosopher by training, could make a single announcement in London that he would be speaking in public on a topic of importance, and people would stop everything to hear him speak. And when he spoke, they would listen approvingly as his knowledge was a source of public admiration. In the United States, the people found little interest in Russell (other than the fact that he had a great deal of money which Americans often find impressive) and regarded him as they would a common person, as their equal. Anyone familiar with Russell and his life would acknowledge at once that he was anything but a common person.[21] Americans are suspicious of reason. It exposes the natural inequalities of human beings in a way that nothing else can.

In as much as the principle of reason is perfected by those who base their lives on the pursuit of wisdom regarding justice (political philosophers), it follows that these same individuals would be most accomplished at living well. To the extent that political philosophers base their lives on perfecting the faculty of reason, they are naturally the most proficient at causing reason to order, direct, and govern their own souls. Political philosophers are masters the art of self-governance, and it follows that they are the individuals who are most free internally. The passion which guides them is the passion to reason, the love of wisdom, philosophy. Socrates, in the *Apology*, defended the life of philosophy before the public tribunal in Athens to such a degree that he placed contemplation as the political ideal in stating:

> and if I say again that the greatest good of man is daily to converse about virtue, and all that concerning which you hear me examining myself and others, and that the life which is unexamined is not worth living—that you are still less likely to believe. And ye what I say is true.[22]

The core of political philosophy is inquiry. This activity is uncommon in democratic times and as a result, the prevailing factor in political behavior tends to be the product of democratic passions: egalitarian public opinion. Opinion of this kind is highly tyrannical in that it militates against free-thought, against reason. Reason pronounces judgment regarding matters of virtue, upon good and evil. And the most prominent distinction is that which differentiates reasonableness from unreasonableness, and mere emotionalism from deliberation. Since political philosophers are most capable of self-rule, they are therefore most capable of ruling others. This is the justification for the rule of philosopher kings which must be taken seriously in our time.[23] The rule of what is right by nature is the rule of reason and that rule requires that those individuals who are most reasonable must govern. The most reasonable individuals in society are the political philosophers, so political philosophers must rightly rule. And their form of rule is congruent with the end of Enlightenment-based constitutionalism in that the basis of the rule of reason is the perfection of the soul writ large, self-government. However much the rule of the wise offends current democratic-egalitarian and relativistic sensibilities, "reason rules the psyche (soul) in a way that is clearly analogous to the way in which the philosopher-kings rule the Kallipolis (polity) (emphasis added)."[24] Justice of the soul translates into social justice. Reason is the principled medium which links disparate and naturally differentiated individuals with each other into one common polity. The glue which fully constitutes a constitutional order, which makes the people whole, is reason. Political philosophers, in living in accordance with the principle of reason as a way of life, are best-suited to rule wisely. Political philosophy provides the positive component of positive self-government which in combination with the negative or preventive forms of the rule of law, complete the dialectic of freedom and equality. Political philosophy assists individuals in living well in there freedom equally before the law.

It is often the case that the one thing most needful for a society is the very thing which that society shuns. In the United States, this one thing is contemplative reason. Reason (as a life ordering, directing, and governing principle) is essentially a deliberative arbiter which regulates the passions. Just as an individual possesses passions, so does a polity. And reason, if cultivated and engaged by way of philosophic education and moral fortitude, distinguishes between necessary desires and unnecessary ones, moderating and governing the soul toward self-sufficiency.[25] This process can be termed "deliberative freedom," the freedom to have and to satisfy only the desires we would choose to have if we were aware of the relevant facts, were thinking clearly, and were free from distorting influences (of the passions) (emphasis added).[26] Deliberative freedom is freedom of the soul which can only occur by way of the regulation of the passions through reason. This requires the influence of political philosophy.

V

How could philosophers potentially rule in a constitutional regime where the many citizens share political power and equality is valued? Must philosophers run for office and attempt to rule directly? Or is there another way in which the wise can have a positive influence in society?

In a constitutional order, the faculty of reason is protected by law.[27] The activity of reasoning (philosophy) is the process of deliberation which makes genuine self-government (responsibility in freedom) possible. Philosophic rule occurs, not through the pursuit of political power (which is unnatural for philosophers), but by way of the cultivation of human hearts, souls, and minds. "Conscientiousness can only be fostered by nonlegal means," that is, by the educational effects of political philosophy.[28] Whereas the law in a constitutional regime creates a sphere of impenetrable freedom where individual natural rights are secured, political philosophy supplies the indispensable role of educating individual citizens in reason, and therefore, responsibility.[29]

The United States Constitution was intended to create a more perfect union (bond) in this way placing primacy upon the public good, upon the interest of society as a whole.[30] Moreover, the framers understood that the first object of government would necessarily be the protection of the diversity in the faculties of men, the most important of which are reason and conscience.[31] To an extent, the *Federalist* was inspired by the classics in so far as the constitutionalism it proposes avoids the perversions of excessive democracy and equality by allowing the natural political ascendancy of those who possess most wisdom to discern, and most virtue to pursue, the common good of society.[32] Publius, in requiring that the laws equally protect individuals in their natural inequality and differences, upholds the Aristotelian ruling principle which "exists in living creatures and originates in the constitution of the universe."[33]

Philosophers may potentially rule in a constitutional order by philosophizing openly, but prudently, in society. Philosophic rule is the indirect, substantially non-legal effect of reason upon the citizenry through education in reason. The rule of philosophers occurs when they do that which by nature they are best fitted to do (which the law expressly protects). In a constitutional regime, the freedom which the law negatively protects must be grounded in responsible self-government through positive education in reason. The philosopher is in this way not obliged to engage in political activity proper, but is:

> responsible to the city only to the extent that by doing his own work, by his own well-being, he contributes to the well-being of the city: philosophy has necessarily a humanizing and civilizing effect.[34]

Political philosophy educates the citizenry regarding the critical importance of utilizing reason to limit the passions, and is in this way, education toward responsible self-sufficiency and self-government. *Philosophers rule in a constitutional order by helping others to rule themselves*. The indirect rule of philosophers in society is the rule of reason, and the rule of reason in a constitutional order is public philosophy.

The effect education in reason will have will differ from individual to individual as it is unrealistic to expect that philosophic education could result in the majority of citizens becoming philosophers. However, it is conceivable that the moderation of unreasonable desires by way of philosophic education could bring about a marked reduction in crimes of passion (such as domestic violence, drug abuse and associated family disintegration, racism, theft/vandalism, gang activity, graffiti, homicide, etc., all of which occur as a result of inner disorder and acting before deliberating). Philosophic education in accordance with the principle of reason might generally consist of the following:

1) Education toward enlightened citizenship (the understanding of the rights and responsibilities of free-living and self-government).
2) Education toward enlightened statesmanship (the understanding of representation in accordance with the Aristotelian principle where the public interest must be given primacy over constituency and self-interest).
3) Education toward enlightened educators (the understanding of reason at each stage of the educational process. The educators of society are parents, role-models, school teachers/college and university professors, religious leaders, etc.)
4) Education toward the cultivation of political philosophers (the understanding of the highest principles of virtue/wisdom in society—public philosophy. Education for those who will make the pursuit of knowledge a way of life).[35]

Political philosophy provides the "independent force" which James Madison neglected, and which positively reinforces a constitutional order. Whereas an extended territory negates majoritarian tyranny, political philosophy provides the essential education (public philosophy) for self-government within the sphere of freedom created by constitutional forms.

The strongest political force in a democracy is public opinion.[36] And since human beings are by nature inclined to speak and act on the basis of partial motives (passion), one role of public philosophy is the questioning opinion, and thereby passion, with reason. By questioning opinion on the basis of reason and the principled interest of society, the tyrannical effects of factions can be further reduced. James Madison's skepticism regarding human nature and the fallibility of reason is well-founded and the idea of utilizing a written constitution to externally guard against tyranny and anarchy (human passions) is based upon sound political analysis. Yet these mechanisms alone lead to a circumstance in which skepticism lapses into cynicism and where the public interest becomes lost in the pluralistic competition of factions for political and governmental control. The negative institutional prevention of injustice must of necessity be augmented by the positive educational, and indeed philosophical, interest of reason. Amidst factional interests in society which mask themselves as the public interest (and which are by definition biased), there must be an independent interest of reason. The need for political philosophy, for the questioning of opinion from the detached perspective of reason, is of critical importance if a constitutional regime is to survive. The "independent force" which Madison associated with "hereditary or self-appointed authority" must actually be located in the role and interest of political philosophy in a constitutional order.[37] Constitutional democracy requires the one thing a democratic people find most difficult to accept: a certain kind of aristocracy, not based upon land ownership or patterns of kinship and descent, but upon the independent role of reason which is the preserve of political philosophers. Political philosophers, in continually concerning themselves with the disinterested pursuit of knowledge and well-being, "found an aristocracy (of reason) within democratic mass society" and in this way civilize a constitutional order.[38] The indirect rule of philosophers resolves at once the crisis of Western civilization as the constitution of philosophic rule is the constitution of public philosophy, and the constitution of public philosophy provides the essential positive pole (freedom "to") of the dialectic of self-government. The constitution of public philosophy is dependent upon the indirect rule of philosopher kings.

Chapter 6

Constituting a Tradition of Reason Upon the Transcendental Standard of Nature

> *Tradition . . . exists as the concrete completion of human nature in a particular society. When truth is experienced within this continuum of social existence and when the experience begets a sense of communion that truth is called tradition. For above all, tradition exists as the experience of truth, as that experience has been progressively developed during the past of a people and carried forward as true to the present, where it is really experienced as true in the soul of each individual member of the community.*
>
> Stanley Parry

In order for public philosophy, the role of reason in society, to be of practical consequence to a people inclined toward radical egalitarianism and relativism, it is essential that it be based upon a standard which transcends the human sphere or plane of existence. Without a transcendental standard, all thought and action must ultimately be closed, and therefore, meaningless. Of course, the absence or neglect of a transcendental standard for society has produced the nihilistic condition which Western civilization and constitutional democracy now confront. The intention of this chapter is to provide a basic outline for and delineate the basic parameters of a transcendental standard for constitutionalism.

I

Walter Lippmann, in his insightful work *The Public Philosophy*, suggested that the modern Western neglect of public philosophy is related to a depreciation of "natural law", a term which has tended to cause considerable semantic confusion.[1] Lippmann's point is certainly worth considering since public philosophy is of necessity intertwined with civic education. The neglect of the natural law aspect of education points toward the heart of the problem, and therefore, the solution. Lippmann wrote:

> Philosophers and scholars and popular educators have relegated the public philosophy to the attic . . . they have treated it as no longer usable by modern and progressive men. It is a neglected philosophy. For several generations it has been exceptional and indeed eccentric to use this philosophy in the practical discussion of public policies.[2]

The modern neglect of public philosophy, and therewith natural law, has produced a void of incredible proportions in the realm of public policy. This problem is central to an understanding and resolution of the crisis of Western civilization as public philosophy is nothing less than the civilizing, moderating role of reason in society.

As Lippmann noted, the term "natural law" is one which is less than clear. As it is beyond the scope of the present enterprise to engage in an extensive discussion of the concept here, it will be sufficient to briefly point out those interpretations of the concept which are impracticable or incompatible with public philosophy in a constitutional order, followed by an articulation of an understanding of the idea which will provide the transcendental standard in question.

As a result of radical egalitarian/relativistic intellectual and moral proclivities in our time, the most common approach to the rule of law is positivism and pluralism. The former derives largely from the objectives and methodology of Enlightenment-based natural science and leads to an either advertent or inadvertent distinction between "facts" and "values". The attempt to make distinctions between facts and values ultimately leads to an associated inability of pronouncing authoritative judgment on matters of public policy. It follows, form this perspective, that all "values" are equal and qualitatively relative or subjective (as only facts can be objectively verified or even falsified).[3] This approach tacitly assumes that the law must be neutral in the face of a pluralistic-democratic (group-based) competition for political power and control which ultimately determines what the law is. Legal positivism and associated democratic pluralism is the ideology which is most pervasive in our time as it is, for example, the predominant approach of the current U.S. Supreme Court.[4]

The fundamental weakness of legal positivism is its neglect of the integral and indeed essential relationship between the law and reason, between law and right (justice). Law cannot simply be neutral. Law must have a purpose and meaning beyond the impassioned struggle for power. And power cannot be taken to be the standard of justice in society unless the Socratically refuted contention of Thrasymachus (i.e., "might makes right") is accepted. To put the matter succinctly, if the law is nothing more and nothing less than the narrowly interested expression of whichever group(s) happen to be predominant at the time, why would it have any authority whatsoever and why would anyone choose to obey it (other than the members of the groups who believe that they might obtain some temporary benefit)? This observation points toward an understanding of the general decline in law-abidingness as a social ideal in the United States and Western democracies generally as the positivistic/pluralistic conception of the law as neutrality has eroded public respect for the law itself. Legal positivism must be placed in contradistinction to natural law as it is ultimately without transcendental foundations. From a natural law perspective, positivism and pluralism are "baseless" and therefore qualitatively base. The law is insufficient by itself.

Natural law has also been interpreted to have a relationship to the "Divine".[5] And yet, the attempt to draw connections between "God's law" or the "word of God" and the law of the land is one which is untenable in a constitutional order. A constitutional society is diverse so that consensus regarding the Divine is impossible to develop. The principle of the separation of Church and State derives from this problematic. For the law to be grounded in the transcendental standard of the "Divine" would require theological singularity which is foreign to a regime based upon the principles of freedom and equality. The law can and certainly must protect the freedom of religion since such is ultimately a matter of conscience.[6] However, appeals to the "Divine" in order to provide justification for the law of the land confront the great difficulty of determining which "Divine" law or code is to be paramount. For this reason, the relationship between right living and the "Divine" must be confined to the private sphere which the rule of law creates and protects (to the extent that this is possible).[7] The Constitution, it follows, cannot be "God's" Constitution, and the "Divine" cannot practicably provide the needed transcendental standard for the law.

II

Intriguingly, legal positivism/pluralism and religious interpretations of the rule of law form the two predominant political poles in many public policy debates in the United States (i.e., the pro-choice Vs. pro-life poles in the abortion debate, or the strong "pro"

Vs. "anti" positions concerning homosexuality). The inability of either side to obtain a social consensus indicates the severity and magnitude of the problem. Legal positivism, which is often associated with extreme views regarding individual rights (often outside of any context of individual responsibilities), has not brought resolution to questions of public policy, and neither has the attempt to invoke the authority of the "Divine" (although this approach at least acknowledges the necessary relationship between the law and right (justice).[8] Failure to find an appropriate transcendental standard for the law has further exacerbated the disillusion Americans feel with respect to government and politics in their society. The so called "grid-lock" is real, and although Enlightenment-based constitutional forms were certainly meant to cause "ambition to counteract ambition", they were not intended to preclude deliberation and eventual agreement regarding the most basic matters and problems of society. Neither legal neutrality nor legal theology can provide the transcendental justification in question.

In a certain sense, the two poles discussed above can be, and often are, referred to as the left (positivism/pluralism) and the right (provisionally termed here—religious constitutionalism). And to the extent these poles become extreme, they mesh together, not ideologically, but in terms of intensity of passion (as opposed to reason) and the propensity to become political or controversial.

The kind of extremism which has evolved from legal positivism (and associated pluralism) can be found in the views of contemporary neo-pragmatists. Richard Rorty, for example, maintains that there is no such thing as transcendental truth or reality:

> But the pragmatist does not have a theory of truth, much less a relativistic one. As a partisan of solidarity, his account of the value of cooperative human inquiry has only an ethical base. . . . For pragmatists, the desire for objectivity is not the desire to escape the limitations of one's community but simply the desire for as much intersubjective agreement as possible, the desire to extend the reference of "us" as far as we can. Insofar as

> pragmatists make a distinction between knowledge and opinion, it is simply the distinction between topics on which such agreement is relatively easy to get and topics on which agreement is relatively hard to get.[9]

Rorty's view reduces all truth to solidarity and group-based agreement. For Rorty, there is nothing but group-based activism and this derives from the anti-intellectual foundations of neo-pragmatism. Note that he discards the philosophic distinction between opinion and knowledge, between passion and reason. Since this position has no epistemological or metaphysical foundation, it is mired in the temporal sphere and in this way cannot admit to a transcendental justification. Rorty concedes this in stating:

> We must, in practice, privilege our own group, even though there can be no noncircular justification for doing so. We must insist that the fact that nothing is immune from criticism does not mean that we have a duty to justify everything.[10]

As is evident, the neo-pragmatism which has resulted from positivistic neutrality is far from neutral. It is bias which has taken the extreme position of asserting that what is true 1) need only be based upon transitory intersubjective agreement and 2) need not be defended by reason.

Neo-pragmatists simply reduce the foundations of society to the politics of agreement and disagreement—irrespective of what is agreed or disagreed upon. What becomes paramount from this perspective is the pluralistic group-based competitive political process proper. The end or goal of society becomes political, controversial. This approach has been taken by certain groups inside as well as outside the American academy. For example, Mark Blasius, in his essay "An Ethos of Lesbian and Gay Existence" contends that:

> politics involves a "*problematization*" or a calling into question of ***power relations*** in society by a social movement through

> *tranformation of techniques* that are *used* to govern people—exercising and submitting to *power relations* (emphasis added).[11]

Blasius views the political sphere, not in terms of an overarching principled ideal which animates and guides society as a whole, but in terms of the politicization of group interests (which by definition are passions) which in his case is the desire to literally transform a traditionally heterosexual society in such a way as to create a lesbian and gay public sphere, "a moral dwelling place made possible through the coming out of lesbian and gay people," and "within which they constitute themselves as ethical beings—as subjects of their actions through erotics—and thereby serve as conditions for the becoming of each other."[12] This is a view from the trenches, one which assumes that the essence of the political is group-based warfare. This grounding of the political in terms of the sub-political is substantially derivative of the positivist interpretation of the law and society which cannot authoritatively pronounce qualitative judgment in the realm of public policy.[13] What remains is passionate human nature expressed without moderation. Directly, without a transcendental justification for the law, groups will make demands upon society in terms of whatever their passionate interest happens to be, and society will be utterly incapable of either affirming or rejecting the expression. The neo-pragmatist position is rooted in the passions, not reason. To the extent that the law is neutral, it must tolerate all opinion so that the passionate interests which are expressed most strongly and with the broadest consensus are upheld irrespective of what their foundations actually are. Usually these desires are claimed to be constitutional rights. Contemporary neo-pragmatism is in this way one cause of the politicization of society and associated political correctness, both of which are the non-relative quasi-absolutist expressions of narrow group interests. Since when could it be plausibly concluded that the unregulated expression of passion, sexual or otherwise, is a constitutional right? This is the condition now facing the post-modern West.

When dogmatic religious belief becomes extreme in the United States it is often asserted to be the inspiration behind the Constitution. It is quite true that America is a predominantly Christian nation and Christianity has been an invaluable source of meaning and support to the polity. Nevertheless, the Constitution cannot ultimately be justified in terms of this tradition for the reasons mentioned above. In fact, history has clearly demonstrated that the mingling of secular law with dogmatic religion has produced tyranny and factionalism as much as any other causal factor.

The will to believe, which is the motivation behind dogmatic religion, while rooted no doubt in plausible faith, is a passion which if unrestrained can lead to serious if not devastating political complications. An example of this phenomenon can be found in the writings and life of Carl Schmitt, the German political theologian who associated himself with the Nazi party as the "Crown Jurist". Schmitt's work represents a modern political-theological reaction to the neutrality and frailty of modern liberalism, one which is instructive in our time. Schmitt was a critic of parliamentary and constitutional democracy as the rule of law is 1) theologically neutral, and 2) based upon the principle of deliberation regarding matters of the first order in society. Schmitt's conceptions of politics and theology were combined to the extent that he reduced:

> the state to a moment of decision, to a pure decision, *not based upon reason and discussion and not justifying itself*, that is, to an absolute decision created out of nothingness (emphasis added).[14]

Beyond noting the close relationship between Rorty's discarding of reason and Schmitt's, it is significant that the latter's conception of politics and the state is anti-deliberative and decisionistic. The "moment of decision" for Schmitt is based upon the most fundamental distinction between friend and enemy. This political distinction, according to Schmitt, occurs upon the foundation of theology and a "normless will."[15] Schmitt attempted to divorce his concept of the political from reason and morality by affirming the political (the friend-enemy distinction—or enmity in terms of theological faith) absolutely.[16] Schmitt's political theology was an illiberal reaction to the "atheistic socialism" inherent in modern liberalism. He was disgusted with a "definitively pacified globe" where entertainment and amusement (as opposed to seriousness) form the basis of existence.[17] Schmitt reacted to the neutrality and frivolity of modern liberalism by developing an anti-thesis of modern liberalism at the level of theological passion which resulted in his demarcating the political in terms of a friend/enemy distinction between German-Catholics and German-Jews.[18] Schmitt politicized his own Catholic theology by severing any distinction between his dogmatic religious belief and politics.

Neo-pragmatism and "politicized" theology often result in the grounding of politics in group enmity. Whereas the pluralism of the left tends to lapse into factional anarchy, the decisionism of the right often results in state-based tyranny (as occurred in Nazi Germany). In as much as tyranny and anarchy are the two most problematic aspects of the human condition, it is clear that neither of these approaches to the rule of law can admit to a practicable remedy for the crisis of constitutionalism. They are both contributing factors to that crisis.[19]

III

As Leo Strauss observed, the Judeo-Christian tradition and the tradition of Classical political philosophy form the basis of Western civilization.[20] These two cultural foundations are each representative examples of the best way of life. And whereas reason has not refuted the position of divinely revealed morality, revelation has not refuted the position of reason.[21] But these two foundations, while similar in many respects, are essentially different as one way is ultimately based upon faith in God's commands, and the other upon faith in pure unassisted human reason.[22] Strauss concluded that the tension and conflict that exists between these two roots provides the cultural vitality of Western civilization. He believed that "no one can be both a philosopher and a theologian," but that "every one of us can be and ought to be either one or the other."[23] Strauss thus attributed the decline of the West to the attempt to synthesize political philosophy with Judeo-Christianity. This synthesis can be discerned in the political theology of Carl Schmitt as well as positivistic pluralism. In the former instance, the state becomes the final arbiter between groups by deciding in favor of one (friend) against the others (enemy) resulting in absolute despotic theocracy. In the latter case, atheistic-positivistic pluralism becomes a secular religion where groups compete for power as a way of life. Directly, Strauss' diagnosis was substantially correct. The attempted synthesis of reason and revelation has weakened both and the West is suffering as a result.

If the Judeo-Christian tradition and the tradition of political philosophy are to be re-established in order to bring much needed vitality to Western civilization and constitutional orders, it will be necessary to provide an appropriate domain for each. This is a matter of considerable consequence in light of the synthesis problematic discussed above. The domain of revealed religion must be confined to the private sphere which constitutionalism creates and protects. Where religion becomes mired in political life both religion and politics are damaged. Once protected (via negative constitutional institutions) freedom of conscience can prove to be highly efficacious in a democratic society. Dogmatic religious belief is useful in a constitutional regime as it causes individuals to look beyond their own self-interest by placing focus and attention upon more distant objects of concern.[24] Alexis de Tocqueville noted that religion tends to have a moderating effect upon democratic passions and this is particularly useful in an egalitarian-relativistic age.[25] Beyond consideration of the utility of dogmatic religious belief in a constitutional order, the Judeo-Christian tradition is based upon the possibility that revealed religion actually offers the answer to the question of the best way of life.[26] Dogmatic religious belief must therefore play a critical role in Western and American life, but this role must of necessity be outside the realm of law (not outside society) and the rule of law if it is to retain its purity and strength.

The transcendental standard for the rule of law can only be ascertained by political philosophy. This derives from the essential relation between natural reason and political right in a constitutional order. The transcendental standard for the rule of law is natural right and the foundation of natural right is reason.[27] Constitutionalism is given meaning by political philosophy as the justification of the rule of law is, and must be, philosophical.[28] Classical political philosophy provides a foundation for politics and society which is not only anti-dogmatic and anti-ideological, but trans-religious and trans-political. Political philosophy is *transcendental* as its object is to move from the realm of opinion to the realm of knowledge via reason. The basic intention of the life of reason is the discovery of the nature of things human and natural, it is the discovery of nature. Reason discloses the transcendental standard of the rule of law which is nature.

The concept of natural law, if it is to serve as the transcendental standard of constitutionalism, must be understood as natural right. Natural right is justice that can be found by human reason to be in accordance with the standard of nature. Natural right, or natural justice, derives from a proper ordering of the nature of human and natural phenomena, from a proper relationship between humanity and nature.

When Rene' Descartes wrote his *Discourse on Method* which placed at the core of the Western world view the primacy of human subjective technological rationality over and above nature, he at once deviated from the inspiration which induced classical philosophers to inquire into the essential nature (eidos) of things natural and human with the desire to fully understand the whole or totality of reality.[29] Now, over three and a half centuries later, while the marked advances technological rationality has made are evident, there is a growing realization that the human attempt to manipulate and dominate nature has produced problems which were unintended, many of which threaten both humanity and nature.[30]

The over-emphasis upon technological rationality (the "How To"?) which was initiated during the Enlightenment Era has caused humanity to cease viewing itself as an integral part of nature. Our post-modern age is plagued with a certain cosmic alienation which is a product of a serious crisis of consciousness.[31] It is imperative that humanity develop an intellectual and moral ecology which is as sophisticated as its technology if natural right is to be cultivated. The present tendency to place primary importance upon the utilization of methodological rationality for the purpose of manipulating and controlling nature in terms of human desires has created an imbalance which is grounded in a disassociation of human thought and practice from the standard of nature. This imbalance has not only effected our natural environment which we rely upon for survival and sustenance by transforming entire ecosystems, changing weather patterns and climates, creating toxic and radioactive waste, as well as holes in the ozone layer of the atmosphere, etc., it has also changed the way in which human beings interact with each other. Human individuals increasingly view each other in terms of calculated passionate self-interest with little if any moderation. Our technological sophistication has come at the price of the quality of living. Western humanity has attempted to control nature prior to having gained control and understanding of itself.

In order for natural right to be upheld, there must be a dynamic interrelation between humanity and nature by way of reason. The relationship between humanity and nature, if properly understood, brings about a natural ordering and balance of human thought and action. The West must acknowledge that the crisis it is experiencing is due to the abandonment of vital natural reason.[32] Contemplative reason assists humanity in understanding the standard of natural right in comprehending what is right or reasonable *by nature*. It is this understanding which Socrates initiated in ancient Greece in living an "examined" life.[33] Natural reason can bring about sobriety and moderation, away from the madness and immoderation of our time.[34] Reason places the human sense of power and mastery which has evolved due to technological-methodological sophistication in proper perspective. It limits the passions by demonstrating the limitation of human understanding by driving home the point that humanity is as an integral component of mysterious nature and not the center of the universe.

Reason discloses the integrated relationship between the human soul, society, and the natural environment. The core of all humanity (East and West) is the soul, and the proper ordering of the soul is contingent upon an appropriate practical and philosophical understanding of the nature of humanity and the relationship between humanity and nature.[35] A provisional definition of natural justice is "the proper intellectual and moral ordering of things human and natural" and the acquisition of natural right is fundamentally contingent upon the development of contemplative reason:

> It is the hierarchic order of man's natural constitution which supplies the basis for natural right. . . . Therefore, the proper work of man consists in living thoughtfully, in understanding, and in thoughtful action. The good life is the life that is in accordance with the natural order of man's being, the life that flows from a well-ordered or healthy soul. . . . The good life is the perfection of man's nature. *It is the life according to nature* (emphasis added).[36]

The life according to nature is the philosophic life. And the philosophic life is the life which is guided, directed, and ordered by reason. Ortega y Gasset well understood that:

> Ours will not be the road that leads over and beyond physics; on the contrary, it will draw back from physics to basic life and find the root of philosophy here. The result will not be metaphysical but ante-physical. It is born out of life itself, and as we will see

> clearly, *life cannot avoid philosophizing*, no matter in how elemental a form. Therefore the first reply to our question, "what is philosophy?" may be phrased thus—"Philosophy is—a thing which is inevitable" (emphasis added).[37]

The transcendental standard of natural right which can only be disclosed by reason or philosophy is, as Ortega y Gasset points out, ante-physical or basic. Human life must of necessity be based upon reason which creates the proper ordering between the physical and the metaphysical. Just as the individual soul must be well-ordered, society must be well-ordered—both in harmony with nature through the dictates of reason. And just as individual justice and social justice are interrelated, they are both a part of nature. Nature is the standard for natural right as it is the basis for balance and moderation. The ancient Greeks understood the wisdom of nature as they, in the words of Jacques Ellul:

> scorned material needs and the improvement of practical life, discredited manual labor (because of the practice of slavery), held contemplation to be the goal of intellectual activity, refused the use of power, and respected natural things. The Greeks were suspicious of technical activity because it represented an aspect of brute force and implied a want of moderation. . . . Here we find the supreme Greek virtue, self control. The rejection of technique was a deliberate, positive activity involving self-mastery, recognition of destiny, and the application of a given conception of life.[38]

The ultimate standard for human life must be philosophy, or the life of reason. There is an unavoidable relationship between human thought and the quality of existence. Ideas indeed do have consequences as the contemporary Western neglect of reason has created a condition of imbalance, discordance, and immoderation. The modern Western over-emphasis upon technological rationality has dulled the sense of wonder which leads to a consideration of the not-self leading beyond and transcending the self. Our time is plagued with selfishness and pride which only reason tempers and restrains. Reason can instill through common sense understanding a cosmic piety which has historically inculcated in humans a necessary element of humility.[39] The order of humanity in accordance with the standard of nature requires the civilizing effect of reason, and "When the individual becomes civilized he acquires a second nature. This second nature is made in the image of what he is and is living for and should become."[40] Post-modern politicization can only be cured by the anecdote of political philosophy.

IV

The constitution of public philosophy, the guiding role of political philosophy in society, necessitates the constitution of the tradition of reason upon the transcendental standard of nature. Walter Lippmann made an important distinction between the first and second nature of humanity. His distinction is based upon the example of Socrates as a model citizen. Lippmann comprehended the essential relationship between public philosophy and political philosophy, and between political philosophy and the standard of nature.[41]

Socrates was "most fully human because he was willing and able to govern his desires," he was a master of self-governance and the ruler of himself.[42] In as much as he ruled his appetites as opposed to being ruled by them, he represented and represents the ideal of the qualitatively best citizen. The quasi-aristocratic virtues which Socrates lived by, are not, as Lippmann pointed out, "inherent in prerogative and birth," but are derivative of the functional capacity to rule.[43] This capacity for self-governance is predicated upon utilizing reason as a principle for life. Socrates took his first nature which was predominated by the passions and by reason developed his second, civilized nature. He moved from the realm of existence to essence, from the sphere of becoming to being. Reason is the principle for well-being upon which Socrates based his life. It is a principle which creates a natural internal and external balance.

Since the political philosopher (the most prominent example of which is Socrates) is a master of self-governance, then this same citizen is most fit to rule in a regime which places self-government as its most cherished ideal (as is the case in a constitutional order). The political philosopher rules indirectly by philosophizing publicly, an endeavor which has an edifying affect on the citizenry. But how exactly is the life and wisdom of the philosopher made publicly effectual?

The answer to this most important question is found in the constitution of a tradition of reason in the form of a code of conduct which evolves into custom or tradition. And the knowledge which this code will convey is "the wisdom of the economy of our passions, and of their education and their ordering." The constitution of reason upon the transcendental standard of nature "does not give the rules of behavior in the actual world," but "it sets before men a vision of themselves transformed."[44] The constitution of a tradition of reason perpetually encourages individuals to become masters of themselves. A tradition of reason forms the cornerstone of constitutional civilization. The practical role of the indirect rule of political philosophy is the establishment of a code of reasonable and right living which eventually becomes the traditional or customary way of life, the public philosophy. The public philosophy of a constitutional order must therefore be based upon the tradition of political philosophy. "Much depends upon the philosophers," for "though they are not kings, they are, we may say, the teachers of the teachers."[45]

V

How can the transcendental standard of nature upon which public philosophy and reason are predicated be understood? This question touches upon a most critical component of public philosophy in a constitutional order. The law must have a transcendental justification in order to be authoritative and the standard of nature which is disclosed by reason provides that support. But nature itself must be understood in such a way as to provide clear guidance on matters of public policy. If reason is to hold justice by nature, it must be indisputable.

The transcendental standard of nature derives from the teleological nature of the universe. Reason discloses this standard by revealing the truth of human existence as "a harmony with the cosmos."[46] The nature of human civilization must be ordered just as physical and biological nature reality are. The code of behavior for civil society must have a transcendental grounding and this is the nature of reality which human reason conveys. The Stoic conception of natural law which Cicero discussed through the voice of Laelius describes this standard:

> *True law is right reason in agreement with nature*; it is of universal application, unchanging and everlasting; it summons to duty by its commands, and averts from wrongdoing by its prohibitions. And it does not lay its commands or prohibitions upon good men in vain, though neither have any effect on the wicked. It is a sin to try to alter this law, nor is it allowable to attempt to repeal any part of it, and it is impossible to abolish it entirely (emphasis added).[47]

What is of critical importance in this view of reason and nature is the combination of wisdom and right, of reason and justice. The probability of wisdom and law coming together is, of course, dependent upon the virtue of a polity and is in most instances highly difficult to obtain. However, the transcendental standard of *right reason* or *natural right* (reason based upon the discovered nature of reality) is permanent. It is either adhered to by good individuals or ignored by ignorant or evil individuals. The standard does not change, irrespective of human folly, and this is precisely why it qualifies as transcendental. Societies approach this standard in a matter of degree. In *The Laws*, Plato's Athenian stranger describes the two motives behind a naturalistic theology which serves to guide a good society:

> One of them is our theory of the soul, our doctrine that it is more ancient and more divine than anything that draws perennial being from a motion that once had a beginning; the other our doctrine of the orderliness in the movements of the planets and other bodies swayed by the mind that has set this whole frame of things in comely array.[48]

The pursuit of truth, which is an arduous discipline in true thinking pursued resolutely to its end and which cannot be divorced from the order of nature around us provides knowledge of the true scale of good and evil by which all humanity must be judged.[49] The understanding of nature (the nature of reality of the first or primary things) requires political philosophy. And political philosophy, by doing its work, provides the proper framework for the ordering of society based upon the standard of the best regime, the regime which most closely approximates the standard of nature. Justice by nature is in this way conveyed to a polity in the form of right reason, which takes its bearings from nature and is translated into a code of behavior, into a natural theology. This natural theology or public philosophy is based upon knowledge of what constitutes the well-being and the common good of a people.[50] The Athenian stranger "takes the political art or science seriously because he acknowledges that there are things which are by nature just."[51] The constitution of public philosophy ultimately depends upon the close relationship between philosophy and politics, between reason and society.

It is commonplace for intellectuals to discard the consideration that the wise should rule and that the life of the philosopher ought to be made an example of the best life in society (they discard the concept of natural right). But to discard this classic perspective is to fail to take seriously the possibility that the best regime must of necessity be in accordance with nature and that human excellence is indeed predicated upon the extent or degree to which human beings live reasonably, by nature. Perhaps this problematic has arisen due to the natural improbability of the coalescence of wisdom and rule. But the improbability of this most essential combination is one thing, and a lapse into the acceptance of the relativistic assertion that natural right is impossible is quite another as the latter contention has never been substantiated.

The perfect city as conveyed in Plato's *Republic* is a city in which philosophers rule by philosophizing. Political philosophy creates the best regime based upon reason which by definition is a city in speech. The argument of the *Republic* is the highest standard, the ideal. This ideal marks the end or goal of humanity by nature and therefore provides the standard for all societies. Whereas the best regime would ideally be one in which everyone lives the philosophic life, societies may be judged on the basis of the degree to which they approximate this goal. The objective of public philosophy, the role of reason in society, must in this way take different forms. It must be conveyed to different polities differently.

Cicero, for example, understood that everyone is not equally equipped to acquire a full understanding of the natural law and equally equipped to by guided by it as most individuals succumb quite easily to "bad habits and false beliefs," to the attractions of pleasure and vice.[52] Whereas the thoughtful life is by nature the standard or ideal of the best life, different individuals and peoples possess different degrees of motivation toward achieving this goal. The American framers approximated the philosophic ideal by constituting the rule of law through reflection and choice.[53] And what is intriguing about that founding is the structured way in which it took place.

The Constitution of the United States was developed deliberatively by a few individuals who were best qualified to found a new nation. From a classical Platonic perspective, just as the soul is tri-part, a good society is as well, consisting of the rulers, the guardians, and the producers. Each of the three classes must do its own work so as to compliment the others in accordance with the ordering principle of reason in the same way that each of the parts of the soul must fulfill its proper function. The structure of individual souls and society must imitate the natural structure of the cosmos in order for "the same opinion (public policy disclosed by reason and based upon the hierarchical, principled standard of nature) to exist throughout society. Each part is informed by reason and is given a role in pursuing the public good.[54] C.D.C. Reeve's analysis of this conception is instructive:

> Platonic education gives the producers cognitive access to a mode of the good, guardians access to a figure of the good, and philosophers access to the form of the good, each of which is the structure of a polis. The form of the good is the structure of the polis in which a philosopher-king believes his ruling desire for the pleasure of learning and knowing the truth would be best satisfied. A figure of the good is the structure of the polis in which a guardian believes his ruling desire for the pleasure of being honored would be best satisfied. A mode of the good is the structure of a polis in which a producer believes his ruling desire for the pleasure of making money would be best satisfied.[55]

The American founding incorporated and constitutionalized the components listed above in 1) constitutionally protecting the freedom of conscience and reason (political philosophy), 2) constitutionally delineating the appropriate modes of representation (statesmanship), and 3) constitutionally protecting the ownership of private property and the acquisition of material wealth (the producing citizenry). A life of pure philosophy is not realistically possible or even worthwhile as philosophy must by nature inform a polity. And the American founding is an example of just such an engagement. A life of public service is also insufficient by itself as it requires purpose informed by reason. And finally, a life of making money is meaningless without providing in some way for more refined needs and desires which can only be found through selfless service and contemplation. In order for each of the classes to live well, they must satisfy the needs of the others while having their own needs satisfied. In so far as the American regime was founded in these terms, it was ordered reasonably in accordance with the standard of nature.

What is often neglected is the extent to which political philosophy is essential for the up-keep of a constitutional order. The moderating and regulating educational effects of reason are of vital importance in maintaining standards of civility and excellence in society. Put differently, if philosophers do not descend back into the cave from which they ascended, or if they are not allowed to, the cave (society) becomes closed and purposeless. The principles which animate society can only be ascertained and communicated by reason in accordance with nature. Natural right therefore requires that political philosophy maintain social order by doing it's own work. When political philosophy thrives, it delineates a public philosophy that provides the balance and direction upon which constitutional order depends.

Derivative of the natural rights tradition of the American founding, political and social scientists often take deliberative democracy to be the standard upon which the Constitution is based.[56] But deliberation alone will not secure the public good since not all individuals or classes reason with equal desire and ability. Genuine deliberation requires a singleness of purpose: the acquisition of wisdom or final knowledge. This pursuit is only genuinely undertaken by political philosophers. To assume that mere debate and discussion in society will produce the truth is to misunderstand the concept of deliberation. Indeed, the main weakness of classical republicanism is the belief that mere political discussion and participation will approximate the public good. Unfortunately, the modern mass media acts largely upon the basis of this position. So long as opposing views are aired, it is believed that the truth will emerge. What often occurs is the exact opposite. Different parties publicly argue on television and radio programs without the least intention of listening to each other or of pursuing the truth. These parties seldom if ever change from their original position through an exchange. Socratic dialogue requires the guidance and participation of political philosophers if it is to enlighten and persuade. Debate for its own sake produces atomization and perplexing confusion regarding matters of public policy. Freedom of speech must be based upon the principle that the purpose of speaking is the pursuit of truth. Mere freedom of expression (acting or speaking so as to reinforce passionate interested opinion) exploits the principle of deliberation.[57] C.S. Pierce was substantially accurate in asserting that "human opinion universally tends in the long run to a definite form, which is the truth," but only if it is perpetually questioned and refined by political philosophy.[58] Deliberative democracy is only deliberative to the degree that public opinion is grounded and refined by reason, and not all human beings reason equally.

VI

In as much as the communication of public philosophy is contingent upon the relative ability of a polity to be open to the voice of reason, the way in which the first principles of a regime are constituted is of particular importance. The argument of Plato's *Republic* represents the ideal of philosophic rule and therefore, a regime in which the speech of political philosophers becomes traditional. But in order for this ideal to be approached, first principles must be communicated through proper education in character over time and generations so that they become a comprehensive civil theology based upon natural cosmology. For this reason, Aristotle's social and political work takes the form of treatises.[59] The institutionalization of public philosophy provides the context for subsequent deliberation. This foundation links the polity with the standard of nature and requires all thought and action to approximate wisdom. In order for reason to rule in a constitutional society, it must be made into a tradition. The philosophic nurture of human nature become the center or core of free, responsible living. A tradition of reason based upon the transcendental standard of nature must be instituted so that constitutional society might be ordered in such a way that each individual and class performs its appropriate function. It is upon the basis of natural right that a constitutional order must be made to exist. Reason and rule must by nature co-exist if the regime that is by nature, the order which provides for both the preservation and perfection of humanity, is to emerge and flourish. A tradition of reason provides the foundation for moral and intellectual development and judgment by properly ordering individual character as well as social interaction in accordance with a non-dual, comprehension of the nature of physical and metaphysical reality. Once reason becomes traditional, it becomes the fundamental basis for the best way of life and gives purpose and meaning to constitutional citizenship. A tradition of reason founded upon the transcendental standard of nature forms a public philosophy which when combined with the rule of law, completes the dialectic of constitutionalism by linking freedom with responsibility.

Chapter 7

Public Philosophy and Citizenship

If a man proposes to give a society laws for the conduct of public and communal life, and yet imagines that law is superfluous when it comes to compulsion in private affairs, that it is improper to submit everything to regulation and that the individual should be left free to spend the day just as he pleases if he leaves personal conduct exempt from legal control and yet flatters himself that his citizens will be ready to guide their communal and public action by law—he is seriously mistaken.

Athenian Stranger
Plato, *The Laws*

Bertrand Russell suggested that the fundamental problem of ethics and politics is that of reconciling the needs of social life with the urgency of individual desires.[1] It would appear that this diagnosis is partly correct but substantially incorrect. True, there is currently a tension between radical, passionate individualism and the public good in the West. However, this tension is not fundamental or essential to ethics and politics. To the contrary, there is *not **by nature*** a tension between individual desires and society, unless raw, untutored human nature is considered to be the standard by which ethics and politics is based. Western humanity has simply deviated from the standard of natural right producing the tension Russell described. Human beings are, as Aristotle discerned, by nature social beings.[2] And the faculty which makes society possible is reason. It is not possible to disassociate what it means to be fully human from social interaction, the highest form of which is reason in the form of speech. Just as no individual is an island, completely independent from others (a condition which requires no speech and no reason), society is based upon the principle of natural right which is most closely approximated by the kind of communication which ties individuals together and assists them in not surviving only, but in living well.

The dualistic tension between individuals and society which pertains in the post-modern West is unnatural and it threatens the vitality and ecology of natural right (the proper ordering of things). Reason, if exercised and consulted, recommends that the full realization of the self is predicated upon a certain degree of selflessness. Individuals in each of the three natural classes of a polity, for example, find significance in existence as social beings. Producers produce not simply for themselves, but for others. Guardians protect and serve in the vision of the interest not simply of the self or a part, but of society as a whole. And philosophers pursue knowledge, not self-indulgently, but for the polity in which they philosophize. Natural right precludes a duality between individuals and society and thereby appreciates them both.

The objective of this chapter is to examine the relationship between individuals and society in terms of public philosophy. The analysis will demonstrate the extent to which a tradition of reason based upon the transcendental standard of nature provides the moral and intellectual foundation for human relations in the form of citizenship. Public philosophy naturally connects individualism with collectivism by grounding both in a way of life (Being) which is rooted in the development of the faculty of reason. Reason causes the dualism between individual desires and the collectivity to dissipate giving way to the creation of a civilized culture. The culture of natural right is predicated upon the cultivation of the human mind.[3] And the cultivation of the human mind produces high civilization, a condition which is characterized by a natural coalescence of human beings.

I

There is a growing concern regarding the decline in civility in Western democracies generally and particularly in the United States. Scholars have often associated the incivility of our time with a certain void in the realm of public virtue.[4] A common diagnosis of the problem traces the decline of public or civic virtue in America back to the tension that exists in American political thought and practice between extended republic nationalism and limited participatory democracy which favors small, autonomous communities—between federalism and anti-federalism.[5] This tension is in part a result of the federal constitutional framework which is largely based upon a skeptical view of human nature, but which is nevertheless considerably reliant upon public virtue. To the present, defenders of federalism and anti-federalism have been at an impasse with the former emphasizing the necessity of regulating democracy and the latter stressing the need for deregulation and local self-government. Lost in this debate is the understanding that both sides are substantially correct but incomplete. Thus Wilfred M. McClay is accurate in pointing out that:

> The challenge is to find ways of restoring the sense of accountability and belonging offered by smaller, more human-scale institutions, institutions that can serve as schools of citizenship, while retaining the very considerable benefits of national government.[6]

What is of vital importance, of course, is the specific articulation of exactly how public virtue can be restored in a federal constitutional regime.

The problematic in question hinges upon the role of government in a free society and this role cannot be fully expounded in temporal-spatial terms. Whereas an extended republic significantly prevents the consolidation of interest into a tyrannical majority and for this reason is preferable to a small, homogenous, democratic republic, the Anti-Federalist concern for the formation of citizen character remains.[7] The Federalist proposal for the creation of "a more perfect union" prevailed, but there is now a discernible disunity between the condition of American citizenship and the animating purpose of the regime. The Anti-Federalist argument, which to a certain extent reflected the idea of a classical republic in which character formation and the principles of the polity are combined, points toward a resolution of the apparent dilemma.[8] The answer, however, cannot be found in confederation.

There is a perceptible loss of a sense of community in the United States which accompanies the marked depreciation of public virtue. The institutions which once formed citizen character and created bonds between individuals appear to be in disrepair.[9] Part of the problem is, undoubtedly, an over-extension of the republic. However, the root of the difficulty is not predominantly territorial, but intellectual and moral. America is experiencing a crisis of public philosophy due to the desperate need for the qualitative independent force of political philosophy. The United States is a nation which is fundamentally animated by certain transcendental principles or ideals. America is an idea which must be conceptualized and communicated properly in the citizenry if the nation is to function well. The activity of ideation is the preserve of political philosophy. Due to a vacuum of political philosophy in the United States, the American idea, the principled good which gives the nation purpose and meaning, has been neglected and in many instances attacked.[10]

The extended republic model actually fosters local autonomy in preventing excessive political and social homogeneity and promoting diversity. In fact, territorial extension was expressly intended to create the conditions for local self-governance. But if the principles which animate the American regime are not perpetually disclosed and inculcated into the citizenry, genuine local autonomy cannot survive. The Declaration of Independence, which articulates to a large extent the inherent truths which guide the nation, stipulates that "all men are created equal" and that they have certain inalienable (natural) rights which governments are instituted to protect.[11] The U.S. Constitution was and is intended to protect the basic rights of individuals in the pursuit of the public good or justice. At a most basic level, the protection of natural rights limits the institution of government as well as the citizenry in order that the citizenry can govern itself to the extent that this is possible. The principle of self-government requires a distinction between a *limited* public sphere which is governed by the rule of law, and an *extensive* private but social sphere which is the domain of self-government. The "pursuit of life, liberty, and happiness" is clearly an engagement in self-rule. Self-government must, however, occur in accordance with a positive transcendental standard which the rule of negative public law cannot fully provide (as the Constitution itself must also be informed by this standard). Put differently, self-government in freedom requires responsibility, demands a sense of duty, and necessitates a life ordering, directing, and governing principle. There "is an essential connection between the *eidos*, the form, the character of a regime, and end to which it is dedicated."[12] That connection in America must be education in reason toward enlightened citizenship, toward responsible citizenship in self-government. Reason naturally fosters individual and therefore collective responsibility. If the citizenry either cannot, or will not govern themselves, something or someone else must. Human life cannot exist in a vacuum and the American regime, which is fundamentally based upon the concept of limited institutional government and extensive self-government, is no exception. Indeed, the American ideal is extremely difficult to attain in that it places the overwhelming share of governmental responsibility on the citizenry proper. American citizenship succeeds or fails to the degree that it is guided by education in reason. This education, once institutionalized, forms the public philosophy which connects the American people to the end to which their regime is directed.

> Every political society derives its character from a specific public or political morality, from what it regards as publicly defensible; and this means from what the preponderant part of society, not necessarily the majority, regards as just.[13]

The preponderant part of American society must be the independent force of political philosophers and those citizens who uphold the standards of responsible self-government. The United States Constitution protects the natural rights of the citizenry, the most important of which is the right to reason. Political philosophers must then educate the citizenry in right reason in order for the connection between the form of the regime and its end to be upheld.

Reinhold Niebuhr observed that:

> The world of history, particularly in man's collective behavior, will never be conquered by reason, unless reason uses tools, and is itself driven by forces which are not rational . . . the easy subservience of reason to prejudice and passion, and the consequent persistence of irrational egoism, particularly in group behavior, make social conflict an inevitability in human history, probably to its very end.[14]

Niebuhr considered humanity astutely. He understood that human beings are initially passionate and unreasonable. But he also believed that the development of reason makes for increasingly just relations between individuals by increasing a sense of moral responsibility while humanizing individuals by purging social relations of as much egoism as possible.[15] This is the challenge of the ideal of self-government, to at once anticipate the pernicious aspects of unrefined human nature while regulating and moderating these forces through proper education in reason. The remedy for a loss of public virtue in the United States is not primarily a structural change, but education in public virtue proper. Structures and institutions cannot, in and of themselves instill public virtue. Education in reason can and must mold not only character, but social institutions and structures as well.

II

Constitutional citizenship requires public virtue of a certain kind. The Platonic synthesis of virtue and wisdom (virtue is wisdom and wisdom is virtue) must be applied. This application is crystallized in an exemplary way of life, the life of the mind.

The discipline which combines virtue and wisdom is political philosophy or science. For this reason, political philosophers contribute to the polity by philosophizing about politics or matters of public policy. Political philosophy, in educating the citizenry in terms of reasonable self-government, provides the essential role of character formation which a constitutional regime demands.[16] The most direct affect this education has on individual citizens is one of encouraging the regulation of passionate desires which are expressed in the form of "opinion" in this way leading toward "knowledge" of self-government and ultimately the good life or the life guided by contemplation.

Public law cannot conceivably be addressed to every aspect of constitutional life. Put differently, everything cannot be legislated, and if it must, self-government is in peril. Constitutional government is limited government and the limitation on government is expressed in the distinction between *state* and *society*.[17] The law which must guide societal self-government is natural law and it is this law which teaches citizens of their duties and responsibilities to themselves and to others.

Citizens are not born, they are made.[18] American citizens, if they are to become truly self-governing, must be educated in such a way that will allow them to overcome their passions, many of which are vulgar and base. This education in reason is liberal education since reason liberates the soul from servitude to untutored desires. This education is provided by the independent force of political philosophy. In the words of Leo Strauss:

> Liberal education is the counterpoison to mass culture, to the corroding effects of mass culture. . . . Liberal education is the ladder by which we try to ascend from mass democracy to democracy as originally meant. Liberal education is the necessary endeavor to found an aristocracy within democratic mass society. Liberal education reminds those members of a mass democracy who have ears to hear of human greatness.[19]

The relationship between political philosophy and the development of constitutional (i.e., self-governing) citizens is essential. Political philosophy is the human activity which is most essential for living well. It is this activity which informs constitutional citizenship. "The political figure of Being, being a citizen, which is apparently one of the most partial and specific modes of being, turns out to be fundamental."[20] When political philosophy informs citizenship it provides what is most essential for human beings in their individual and social capacities.

The best example of the practical relationship of political philosophy to citizenship is provided by the life of Socrates. For Socrates, "to be a citizen was a way of being among others as *zoon politikon*, as political being." For him, "to be was to be among men" and "not to be among men was not to Be as a human."[21] Partly for this reason, Socrates refused to escape his obviously wrongful punishment of drinking the hemlock by fleeing into exile.[22] Note that Socrates did not separate his way of life from his Athenian citizenship. To the contrary, he maintained that his way of life was the best way of life, not only for him, but for all Athenians. Socrates life was the life of the best citizen. He defended philosophy in his polity to the death. He never deviated from his claim that "the unexamined life is not worth living" and he even stated that if possible, he would continue to philosophize in the afterlife.[23] The *Apology* of Socrates revealed the intricate interrelation between philosophy and the polis, between reason or wisdom and citizenship or public virtue. Upon receiving his sentence, Socrates stated:

> When my sons are grown up, I would ask you, 0 my friends, to punish them; and I would have you trouble them, as I have troubled you, if they seem to care about riches, or anything, more than about virtue; or if they pretend to be something when they are really nothing—then reprove them, as I have reproved you, for not caring about that for which they ought to care, and thinking that they are something when they are really nothing. And if you do this, I and my sons will have received justice at your hands.[24]

Socrates is an example of the best citizen because his way of life is the one which citizens should aspire toward living. The life of reason combines reason and virtue in the person of a citizen by perfecting the inner self, the soul. The polity in which one lives is indistinguishable from the mode of life which the regime is directed toward. In a constitutional regime where the objective is self-government, the life of reason, of self-government *par excellence*, is the mode of constitutional living. To be fully human is to be a citizen.[25] And conversely, good citizenship is based upon the most essential of human activities, contemplation. Constitutionalism protects and preserves natural right, and citizens of a constitutional regime in turn positively exercise their right to live by the dictates of reason.

III

Americans have a contempt for traditions and forms, but it is a tradition based upon the forms which reason recommends which they are most in need of.[26] Formality and tradition is partly established in the rule of constitutional law and partly by public philosophy. The control of our actions by intelligence is what is of ultimate importance to human civilization.[27] The formation of character limits the irrational or unreasonable passions of the soul and is therefore indispensable to a constitutional regime. James Q. Wilson understood the issue in noting that:

> The great puzzle for a free society is how it can encourage those traits of character on which the wise exercise of freedom depends. Our Constitution is silent on this matter, and so were, for the most part, the deliberations of the founders. Creatures of the Enlightenment, these men took for granted the existence of sufficient virtue among the people to make free government possible.[28]

Human nature does not automatically possess, or even naturally grow toward, self-rule by reason. The proper remedy for the natural disorder of the soul is the inculcation of habits of self-control beginning when children are very young.[29] William J. Bennet has continually stressed the need to provide citizens, and particularly the youth, with positive habits and ideas.[30] Bennet's training in political philosophy undoubtedly provided him with the following insight:

> Nature abhors a vacuum; so does a child's soul. If that soul is not filled with noble sentiments, with virtue, if we do not attend to the "better angels of our nature," it will be filled with something else. . . . Government, obviously, cannot fill a child's (or an adult's) emotional, spiritual, or moral needs. Government is not a father or a mother. Great as it might be, government has never raised a child. And it never will (emphasis added).[31]

The role of political philosophy in a constitutional order is then one of communicating the principles of self-mastery, and therefore, constitutional citizenship. These principles are then taught in homes, schools, and communities. And, most importantly, once the public philosophy becomes traditional and formalized, it becomes the basis upon which approbation or blame are socially distributed. In light of the fact that human beings are, in the first instance, passionate and irrational, it follows that the public philosophy can encourage or discourage certain kinds of behavior and expression on the basis of public, community based sentiment.[32] Honor and shame are strong incentives in human beings. The realm of constitutional ethics and morals must then be based upon the development, inculcation, and preservation of the manners and customs which are conducive to the public philosophy (which is in turn informed by reason in accordance with the standard of nature).[33] And the ethos of a constitutional society can and must be uniform since it is rooted in the transcendental standard of natural right.

The uniformity of the standard for constitutional citizenship derives from the teleological nature of the universe and the relation of humanity or human nature to that order. There is a direct interrelation between the best way of life, by nature, and citizenship in a constitutional regime. Leo Strauss' examination of classic natural right produced the following observation which succinctly conveys the standard for constitutional citizenship and being:

> It is the hierarchic order of man's natural constitution which supplies the basis for natural right as the classics understood it. In one way or another everyone can be forced to admit that he cannot, without contradicting himself, deny that the soul stands higher than the body. That which distinguishes the human soul from the souls of the brutes, that which distinguishes man from brutes, is speech or reason or understanding. Therefore, the proper work of man consists in living thoughtfully, in understanding, and in thoughtful action. The good life is the life that is in accordance with the natural order of man's being, the life that flows from a well-ordered or healthy soul. The good life simply, is the life in which the requirements of man's natural

> inclinations are fulfilled in the proper order to the highest possible degree, the life of a man in whose soul nothing lies to waste. *The good life is the perfection of man's nature. It is the life according to nature.* One may therefore call the rules circumscribing the general character of the good life "the natural law." The life according to nature is the life of human excellence or virtue, the life of a "high-class person," and not the life of pleasure as pleasure (emphasis added).[34]

The classical political philosophers discovered the standard (natural right) which is the foundation not simply for their time, but for all time. The relationship between natural right and constitutionalism is vitally elucidated in terms of citizenship. A constitutional regime is based upon the rule of law which first and foremost protects natural right. In this way, the best citizen is the individual who lives most closely in accordance with the best life by nature, the life of "human excellence or virtue," the life of reason. This is the context for constitutional citizenship. Book IV of Plato's *Republic* concludes that justice is doing one's own business, and not being a busybody.[35] In constitutional language the Platonic definition of justice translates into the conclusion that justice is the achievement of genuine self-sufficiency or self-government. Constitutional citizenship associates individuals in the common cause of living well. To the degree that individuals can live well, a constitutional society approaches the standard of natural right, of justice. The culture of constitutional citizenship is the culture of the individual and social mind. Constitutional citizenship is based upon the attainment of human excellence, of high civilization.

IV

Constitutional citizenship, while based upon the cultivation of human excellence in the form of reasonable living, must be limited and specific. Directly, Constitutional citizenship in the United States must be American citizenship. There must be a connection between human excellence generally and it's specific pursuit and attainment in America. Constitutional citizenship cannot be "universal" even if the principles which animate it are. This derives from the fact that 1) there is not a constitutionalized global human polity, and 2) constitutional citizenship, which is fundamentally grounded in an organic qualified way of life or Being cannot function in a pluralistic, fragmented, hyper-individualized, and all-extensive mass society. It requires "the confines of community, at subsidiary levels, and therefore, meaningful devolution."[36]

The context of constitutional citizenship in the United States must be grounded in American public philosophy, the unique role of reason in the American polity. The crisis of American public philosophy can be seen in the growing instability of public sentiment, behavior, and discourse. Stephen Bertman has remarked that:

> the original ideals of classical civilization have been inverted by our (American) society . . . self-sacrifice by selfishness; moderation by excess; rationalism by rationalization; honor by greed.[37]

Indeed, the concept of culture as the cultivation of reason which forms the basis of constitutional citizenship has been reversed in contemporary American life to actually mean de-culturation in terms of everything reason is not, in terms of unreason or democratic-egalitarian mass, vulgar passion. The growing decadence of America corresponds to the decrease in civility. American life is no longer characterized by safety, law-abiding peace, and order as "more and more Americans are forced to live in compounds behind locked gates and electronic sensors and security alarms" as the essential codes and conventions that ensured civilized life have been attacked and deconstructed.[38] The "counter-culture" (a culture which is based upon opposition to culture, to the cultivation of the mind) in America, which has its roots in the academy, has largely succeeded in freeing a good number of Americans of intellectual and moral obligations. Public virtue is, as a result, in severe shortage in the United States.

At one time, educational institutions in America taught discipline and self-denial with the understanding that these skills are essential to the perfection of human beings and the development of enlightened citizenship.[39] The pedagogical approach which has prevailed over the last few decades in the home and schools has, however, assumed that it is wrong to require children and young adults to do anything they do not desire to do, including sitting quietly in the classroom or church.[40] It is not an over-statement to suggest that there is at least a generation of Americans who are simply incapable of sustained deferment of instantaneous gratification. This is exhibited through juvenile crime, teen-age pregnancy, drug abuse, and various other forms of self-indulgence. For these individuals, human life is mere existence, without reason.

Many intellectuals who inhabit the academy are actually teaching students that truth and value are entirely relative which has led to a serious depreciation of evaluative reasoning as well as a passionate, hedonistic individualism which results from the identity crisis that is brought on by an ideological outlook which bears no relation to reality and distorts the faculties which engender understanding, precluding genuine self-realization. It is not uncommon to find academics contending that there is no manner in which to qualitatively differentiate (by reason) between "rap" and Mozart for example, as both are viewed to be merely different forms of "expression". Another popular view expounded in the academy holds that "graffiti" is a legitimate and worthwhile form of rebellion against society and tradition.[41]

The identity crisis which has resulted from the void of reason in American public and private life is increasingly taking the form of passionate behavioral extremes. Radical individualism is the outcome of a disassociation from nature and, therefore, reason which results in the need for public expression. Americans are now, for example, permanently tatooing, piercing, and branding themselves (the latter entails burning human flesh with a red-hot iron which is heated to 1,100° F) in order to express rebellion and differentiation, a practice which many academics find to be a unique form of individualism.[42] Ironically, these behaviors are indicative of a herd mentality. Allan Bloom was correct in asserting that true diversity is never found in the mere pursuit of diversity.[43]

V

American citizenship must be grounded in public philosophy. And whereas citizens are "born" free as a result of the institution of the rule of law (a written constitution), they must be "made" Americans. Public philosophy in the United States requires that citizenship be tied to the principles of natural right where individuals learn to live reasonably and to govern themselves well individually and collectively.[44] Where reason serves as a life ordering, directing, and governing principle, the negative aspects of human nature are regulated by law while character is positively molded by custom and tradition. Reason completes the dialectic of a constitutional order in creating what the classics called a *politeia*, a constitution of what is more fundamental than the law as it is the source of all law and the foundation of the best society.[45] An American *politeia* is the moral and intellectual foundation for the American way of life (Being). The constitution of an American *politeia* incorporates public philosophy in the formation of American citizenship. The American *politeia* is ordered in accordance with the standard of natural right so the refined desires of individuals are conducive to the public good, and the public good is conducive to the refined desires of individuals. Public philosophy is necessary for enlightened citizenship just as wisdom is necessary for living well. The constitution of an American *politeia* unites citizenship with a form of being, the best form of being, with the life of reason.

Perhaps the greatest American Statesman, Abraham Lincoln, expressed concern over the need for the American citizenry to feel an attachment to their way of life and Government. He comprehended the extent to which this strong feeling, which is the bulwark of any society, is associated with law-abidingness, with the capability of a people to govern themselves.[46] Lincoln acknowledged that the history of the American revolution could not support the bonds of citizenship based upon freedom, equality before the law, and self-government as time gradually erases the memory of such events. The emotional consciousness of the nation's historical origins would need to be replaced by a stronger, everlasting force:

> They were the pillars of the temple of liberty; and now that they have crumbled away (the memories of the revolution), that temple must fall, unless we, their descendants, supply their places with other pillars, hewn from *the solid quarry of sober reason. Passion* has helped us; but can do so no more. *It will in the future be our enemy. Reason*, cold, calculating, *unimpassioned reason*, must furnish all the materials for our future support and defense. Let those materials be moulded into general intelligence, sound morality and, in particular, a reverence for the constitution and laws (emphasis added).[47]

Abraham Lincoln's *Gettysburg Address* culminated in the re-dedication of the nation to "the proposition that all men are created equal" and to "the great task remaining before us" of securing a "new birth of freedom" in the protection of "government of, by, and for the people."[48]

Public Philosophy serves to accomplish the great task Lincoln envisioned for the American nation in providing the foundation of citizenship in equality, freedom, and self-government. If America is to survive, each citizen must, to a certain degree, live reasonably, as reason forms the core of the culture of a free people. A *Politeia Americana* is distinguished not by class, blood-lines, or ancestral customs, but only by a tradition of civility which is the product of the reasoned cultivation of the heart, soul, and mind. Reason is the civic religion of American citizenship.

Chapter 8

Public Philosophy and Public Policy

We need wisdom most when we believe in it least. If the new nature of our acting then calls for a new ethics of long-range responsibility, coextensive with the range of our power, it calls in the name of that very responsibility also for a new kind of humility.

Hans Jonas

Public philosophy is the role of wisdom or reason in the life of a polity. If it flourishes, it informs the laws and customs of political life in the form of public policy. What is evident in the United States today is a profound confusion regarding public policy symbolized by either self-indulgent apathy or group-based pluralistic confrontation and disagreement over the most basic of issues in public life. This socio-political malaise is substantially derivative of the poverty of public philosophy. Laws and customs must be grounded in reason, not simply passionate opinion, if they are to be meaningful and it is this justification which is absent presently.

The current crisis of public philosophy can be surmounted if the transcendental standard of nature is re-established as the foundation for developing the reasoned explanation for public policy. We have, in post-modernity, discarded nature and it is this standard which can provide the solution to our current problems. By utilizing the faculty of contemplative reason, we can begin to live *with* nature and not against it. This is not to say that we should live instinctually in the Darwinian sense. Reason is a regulating and moderating force which is essential to living compatibly with nature and therefore, with each other. To live with nature via reason is to comprehend the need for ecological balance. Public policy should, above all else, serve to establish a natural ecology between humanity and nature.[1]

There is considerable resistance in our time to the idea of returning to the traditional relationship that humanity once had with nature in the pre-technological age. Of course, this insolence is the product of the discarding of reason and is symptomatic of the crisis in which we are enveloped. Indeed, since the Enlightenment humanity has not experienced itself as an integral part of nature.[2] For this reason, our post-modern age is mired in a sense of cosmic alienation, the product of a profound crisis of consciousness.[3] We have placed pragmatic methodology over contemplative reason so that practice guides our principles instead of the other way around. Thus, we are no longer inspired with the awe which induced Classical philosophers to inquire into the essential nature (eidos) of things natural and human with the desire to genuinely understand the world and the place of our existence within it.[4] As a result, our social-political institutions are in disarray.

The intent of this chapter is to examine the relationship between public philosophy and public policy as it applies to political life in the United States. Once political philosophy is brought to bear on issues of public policy, a natural ecological order (both legal and customary) can be established which will fully integrate individuals with their polity and environment in terms of reason resulting in socio-political justice writ large. The recovery of the transcendental standard of nature via reason provides the formula for instituting public philosophy and informing public policy in a constitutional order. This is the foundation which completes the dialectic of constitutionalism by combining negative freedom with positive responsibility. The analysis which follows lays a general and rudimentary foundation for public policy in constitutional orders and America in particular.

I

The strong American tradition of rights based thought and the separation of church and state as well as the public and private spheres precludes the utilization of law to directly articulate public philosophy. The law, in the negative-constitutional sense, serves primarily as a preventive agent. Direct reasoned prescription must therefore be rooted in the positive development of customs which inform public virtue and self-government. The law can and must support the public philosophy once it becomes an integral part of the citizenry's practice. The public philosophy in a constitutional order is fundamentally intellectual but its practical expression is ethical or moral. "'Ethics' is drawn from the Greek *ethos*, meaning 'custom,' and "moral' traces back to the latin *mos*, *mores*, meaning 'custom(s),' 'manner(s).'"[5] The public philosophy is freely practiced in a constitutional regime by the people as a way or manner of life which points toward the public good.

The development of a practical role for wisdom in American life confronts a number of obstacles. America is a nation which was born out of a break with tradition and which is therefore rooted in a tradition of anti-traditionalism.[6] It is also a polity which is based upon the principle of popular democratic government which places public policy debate and decision in the realm of majoritarian public opinion as opposed to the authoritative customs handed down by an aristocratic elite.[7] The American people are, as a general rule, pragmatic in their outlook. That is, they tend to shun ideas, forms, philosophy, in favor of practical methods of thought making the abstract formality of custom and manners somewhat foreign to their tastes.[8] And finally, Americans value equality to the extent that they are disinclined to pay respect to the views of a select number of individuals on the basis of their virtue and knowledge (in this instance, political philosophers).

Nevertheless, American constitutionalism secures a great degree of freedom, including that of conscience, which suggests that where there is sufficient will on the part of the citizenry to live in a certain manner, there is a way. Indeed, if the people of the United States become cognizant of the intricate relationship between public philosophy and free self-government, they might very well be inclined to adopt the traditions of civility which will perpetuate their unique condition. In order for U.S. constitutionalism to survive and prosper, political philosophy must be made practically effectual—it must inform the practice of free-living, it must guide and direct public policy.

In order to delineate the specific public policy directives which public philosophy in a constitutional regime might recommend, it is necessary to make reference to Classical political philosophy. Aristotle begins *The Politics* intriguingly, by discussing the nature of humanity and the relationship between human nature and the structure of the household, community, and polity as a whole.[9] He utilizes the phrase "by nature" throughout his work as he did not believe that the state or polis is an artificial creation. On the contrary, he utilized the transcendental standard of nature in order to take his bearings in examining politics and public policy. For this reason, Aristotle does not place primacy in concepts such as power, control, equality, representation, or tolerance since the "nature of things" human and natural recommend a distinct ecological-hierarchical ordering.

It is here appropriate to put forward a social-political ordering of human affairs in accordance with nature. Not unlike *The Politics*, this ordering will be both explanatory and prescriptive, thereby unifying a coherent public philosophy with basic general standards of public policy. Aristotle asserts that "the state belongs to the class of objects which exist by nature," and that "man is by nature a political animal."[10] If human beings are by nature such that they must live together (in a polity), then the radical egalitarianism and individualism of our time is contra nature, it is misguided.[11] This is an important starting point for re-shaping the ecological order of political life in the United States since the excessive valuing of equality and individualism have led to the gradual deterioration of the basic institutions of society.

The most fundamental and natural of social institutions is the relationship between man and woman, marriage. This institution is in disrepair, largely due to radical egalitarianism and individualism. By nature, men and women are different (biologically, etc.) but naturally compatible in their differences. Their differences naturally complement each other in forming the most essential of social bonds. If nature is referred to as the standard for marriage, there will be a hierarchical structure to the interaction and a pronounced division of labor. This ordering is functional as it does not contravene the nature of things. Unfortunately, as nature has been discarded as a standard in our time and has been replaced by egalitarianism and individualism, the structure of marriage and the relationship between men and women has become leveled and atomized.

In the words of James Fitzjames Stephen, "equality has no special connection with justice, except in the narrow sense of impartiality."[12] Equality before the law is one thing, whereas absolute equality in terms of social interaction and relationships is quite another. Individualism, if pushed to the extreme, conflicts with human nature, with the Aristotelian observation that we are by nature social. Marriage forms the foundation upon which humans build other social bonds and humans instinctively understand that the strength of their communities is dependent on the strength of their marriages.[13] However, the egalitarian view of marriage combined with excessive individualism has brought disunity to the relationship. When marriage partners consider themselves to be equals, the institution fails when they disagree as neither individual plays a final decision-making role where determinations are made by reason in the interest of the marriage. By not placing the good of the marriage or union first, equal individuals engage in cost-benefit analyses in order to determine whether their own self-interest can best be served by remaining true to the institution. This often leads to divorce (approximately 50% of the time in accordance with the principle of equality). When half of the marriages in society fail on average, this indicates that an extremely large proportion of the society at large is in disarray at any given time. No society with a high divorce rate can survive for successive generations. And yet, this is a condition which afflicts America presently. The price of radical egalitarianism and individualism is in this case the demise of the most important cornerstone of a free society.

The difficulty post-moderns have in ordering their social relations is largely derivative of the modern Enlightenment-based attempt to place humanity above nature, individuals above society or the state, and equality above teleology. Aristotle placed at the core of his *Politics* the standard of nature. He maintained that "every state exist by nature" and the aim of the state is self-sufficiency or perfection.[14] Aristotle's political science acknowledged that the sharing of a common view of good and evil, just and unjust, etc. "makes a household and a state."[15] And, most importantly, his teleological conception of nature caused him to assert the following principle: "the whole must be prior to the part."[16]

It is this principle, that the whole is prior to (meaning that it takes primacy over) the part, that brought Aristotle to suggest that the purpose of civil society is the perfection of humanity. Since nature does nothing without some purpose, the state must have a purpose, and this purpose is the development and improvement of humanity.[17] The perfection of humanity requires the inculcation of virtue.

> For as man is the best of all animals when he has reached his full development, so he is worst of all when divorced from law and justice. . . . Hence man without virtue is the most savage, the most unrighteous, and the worst . . . for justice is the arrangement of the political association, and a sense of justice decides what is just.[18]

The natural rights which a written constitution secures must be sustained by an appropriate arrangement of the political association and civic virtue. The virtue Aristotle is considering is one which is grounded in natural reason.[19] In referring to George Washington's Aristotelian conception of political principles, Charles Kesler writes:

> man's possession of reason distinguishes him from the beasts, but his imperfect possession of reason . . . distinguishes him from the divine being, the kind of being whose rationality is perfect and unaffected by desire. As the in-between being, man's dignity derives from his place in this ordered universe. The rights of man are governed by man's nature, which means *man's place in nature*, which means the natural law (emphasis added).[20]

Genuine personhood in a constitutional order is dependent upon ritual. Ritual sets a context for person-making, for the inculcation of virtue which develops reason and civility (the capacity for self-government).[21] Ritual "provides a context for acting freely," and "has cosmic ground in which the universe is at stake; ritual has cosmic efficacy."[22] Ritual provides a traditional cultural paradigm for person-making which is achievement oriented.[23] Every individual in a free society is a human individual, but personhood requires certain achievements. The ritual which symbolizes person-making in a constitutional order is *citizenship*. "Good citizenship involves more than simply a quid pro quo for the state's protection. It requires that those whose citizenship depends on the rights of man conduct themselves as *human beings*."[24] Citizenship is contingent upon individuals showing themselves capable of governing themselves and their passions by reason in accordance with nature. The purpose or aim of a free society is civilization expressed through the rite of citizenship. "In the Founders' view, American citizenship and civility were distinguished by their dedication to the common purpose of Western civilization."[25]

The cultivation of reason is the most important component of the ritual of citizenship. Russell Kirk noted that Socrates,

> was a great moralist; his aim was to make philosophy an ethical study once more, rescuing it from the pit of abstract speculation . . . and from the sophistical pursuit of power. Socrates and his pupils agree, the wise man is the good man, and the good man is the wise man. Socrates believed the end of learning to be ethical, and that right reason would support the cause of virtue.[26]

By reason, if each individual is master of himself/herself, then the family, community, and state will also exhibit this same feature.[27] This is why Socrates concluded his *Apology* by requesting the citizens of Athens to raise his sons to live virtuously.[28] Socrates was a champion of philosophic education as the rite of passage toward enlightened citizenship.

What is then the correlation between the need for sound marriages and households, education in reason in the development of citizens, and the transcendental standard of nature? Nature recommends that the institution which is fundamentally responsible for the production and cultivation of citizens in a free constitutional regime is first and foremost the household. It is, therefore, of critical importance that households be properly arranged, by nature. The proper arrangement of households will 1) best preserve the family, 2) best lead toward the improvement and happiness of family members, and 3) best instill in children the virtues of citizenship in the form of customs or traditions. Citizens are not born, they are made.[29] And the institution which is primarily responsible for citizen-making is the household.

Public philosophy must inform public policy by setting down traditions regarding marriage and the household which are consented to by the citizenry and to which stigma's are attached in order to provide appropriate incentives.[30] These traditions, such as marriage and family governance support and are supported by laws, but are ethical standards which guide citizens in the domain of free self-government:

> traditions should neither be designated laws nor left unformulated. They are the mortises of a constitution, the connecting links between all the enactments already reduced to writing, and preserved by it . . . a true *corpus* of ancestral and primitive tradition which, rightly instituted and duly followed in practice, will serve as a sure shield for all the statutes.[31]

The establishment of public philosophy specifically requires the setting down of traditions which guide public policy. Whereas marriage and family matters are often deemed to be "private" affairs in our time, what is often over looked is their political nature. Marriage and the household are by definition social institutions since they involve more than one individual and are inextricably linked to the preservation and improvement of individuals.

At the core of public philosophy is the cultivation of character by way of appropriate training and education. The cultivation of character is essential for the process of self-governance and therefore free-living. Families are the single most important factor in the socialization of children toward enlightened, responsible citizenship (note, for example, the extent to which parental teaching of the principle of equality embodied in the *Declaration of Independence* would serve to reduce racism).

Johannes Althusius pointed out that certain political writers wrongly eliminate the doctrine of the conjugal and kinship private association from the field of politics, not recognizing that these associations are the seedbed of all private and public associational life.[32] The household is a private association that is inextricably linked to the preservation and well-being of the polity, it is a political association which serves to promote the ritual of citizenship. Families not only propagate the human species, they "are the primary socializing agent for children." Wade F. Horn's perspective on the matter is worth citing at length:

> Proper socialization requires the development of the ability to delay or inhibit impulse gratification in order to follow the rules of society. Well-socialized children have learned not to strike out as others to get what they want; undersocialized children have not. Well-socialized children have learned to listen to and obey the directions of legitimate authority figures, such as parents and teachers; undersocialized children have not. Well-socialized children have learned to cooperate and share with others; undersocialized children have not. In short, well-socialized children have developed the ability to self-regulate impulse gratification; undersocialized children have not. Much of what is described as good character or virtue reflects this ability to delay or inhibit impulse gratification.[33]

It is important to note that households produce citizens, and also that it is parents, marriage partners, who perform this important task. Whereas children are brought up to be good citizens in the household, this process is largely contingent upon the character of the parents themselves. Good citizens must be cultivated by good citizens.

II

What specifically should the traditions of civility direct in the case of marriage and the household—by nature? Here the analysis takes on a form similar to that found in Plato's *The Laws* in which certain behaviors are customarily either approved or disapproved and which is seemingly foreign to post-modernity. In an egalitarian/

individualistic age, pronouncements of reasonable standards which limit desires and which are not subjectively relative are often disregarded. But standards are standards and the standard of nature transcends passionate relativism. St. Thomas Aquinas pointed out that law is from reason. For all humanity this is one and the same, and there is but one single precept of natural law.[34] Hadley Arkes made the argument for ethical standards which are grounded in nature and understood via reason as follows:

> If we look up virtuous, it refers to what is "good" or "right"—and on it goes. The exercise does not prove that definitions are circular; nor does it prove that "the good" is indefinable. It merely means, I suggest, that we are in the presence of *primary terms*, which are built into the logic of our language and "the constitution of our natures." At some point, all definitions must find their origin in words that cannot themselves be defined. Otherwise, how could we know the words used in the *first* definition? We must acknowledge certain terms which are needed in building our understanding of other words and concepts; and the words associated with morals—good and bad, right and wrong, just and unjust—are among those irreducible terms.[35]

The justification of the public, philosophical articulation of ethical standards is that they are "by nature" derived from reason period. They are such that no *reasonable* human being would reject them, for so doing would mean to contravene what it means to be human.

What follows is a specific delineation of some of the basic points of marriage and household policy which should become traditional in a free constitutional order:

1. Marriage should be made an institution of central importance in society. It should be taken seriously and should become the standard for the fulfillment of citizenship. Divorce should be made the exception to the rule. Social stigma's should therefore be attached to divorce and marriage should be free of dissolution absent extra-ordinary circumstances.[36] Treating marriage within the context of the principle of equality places the institution in serious danger of collapse. This places individuals above the union and men above women since after divorce, the living standards of women and children tend to drop, often dramatically, while the living standards of men tend to rise.[37] Within marriage differences between wives and husbands should be accentuated in accordance with the standard of nature resulting in a dialectical unification based upon role differentiation. Decisions should be made jointly with the man serving as the final arbiter making final decisions based upon the interest or good of the marriage and household (as opposed to self-interest). Male household leadership should be based upon the prerequisites of self-mastery (particularly with respect to the sexual passions) and the concept of "leading by serving".

Men and women should be encouraged to marry, but only once they are mature and prepared to take upon themselves social responsibility. Marriage and household maintenance are responsibilities which both men and women should bear together in society. The obligations and fidelity which accompany these institutions serve to regulate the passions and channel them in appropriate, respectable ways. The utmost respect should be paid to responsible fatherhood and motherhood.

Men and women should be trained in etiquette and educated in the principles of self-government (citizenship) so that these same manners and understandings can be inculcated in their children. Morals and manners are not conflicting, but are complementary. In the words of Judith Martin:

> no one has yet come up with a satisfactory substitute for family etiquette training in the earliest years of life to foster development of the child in such manners principles as consideration, cooperation, loyalty, and respect and to teach the child such etiquette techniques as settling disputes through face-saving compromise. . . . A society can hope to function virtuously only when it also recognizes the legitimacy of manners.[38]

2. Monogamy must be idealized. Sexual relations outside of marriage should be forbidden and a strong stigma should be attached to extra-marital sexual intercourse. This policy not only preserves the faith and trust which is essential to the stability of marriage, it prevents premature sexual activity in youth as well as irresponsible pregnancy (pregnancy outside of marriage is a serious social malady as it lacks the structural support of *both* father and mother as well as the community).

3. Pregnancy must be understood to be, "by nature," the product of sexual intercourse between a man and a woman who are married for life. Moreover, even though sexual intercourse can be engaged in for both procreation and pleasure, it is a natural fact that absent extra-ordinary circumstances, this act can potentially produce pregnancy. For this reason, sexual intercourse must be restricted to partners in marriage.

4. From the stipulation that pregnancy is a product, by nature, of sexual intercourse, it follows that consent to engage in sexual intercourse (within or without the bonds of marriage) is also tacit consent to be responsible for the implications and results of that intercourse. Therefore, pregnancy is the responsibility of the man and the woman who consent to and engage in sexual intercourse (again as a matter of policy, within the bonds of marriage). The primary share of the responsibility (equality is not the operative principle of policy) is the man's, but the responsibility is shared within the marriage union.

5. It follows that abortion (absent the extra-ordinary circumstances of rape, incest, potential harm to the mother, and serious fetal defects and abnormalities) must as a policy be forbidden. A stigma of irresponsibility should be attached to abortion. Whereas married couples can engage in family planning, utilizing various methods of birth control including abstinence, abortion must be viewed as an act of selfishness and a breach of duty. Abortion is *contra* nature and therefore unjust. A pregnant woman has no right by nature to do whatsoever she pleases to herself in this instance as she voluntarily engaged in the action which precipitated the pregnancy. A man who has caused a pregnancy is not only responsible, by nature, for the product of his action, he also must be made responsible for the woman who carries the child in marriage. Again, for this reason, extra- and pre-marital sexual relations must be forbidden and deemed as irresponsible.

Procreation cannot be taken lightly in civil society as human beings require many years of sustenance and tutelage. Childbearing outside the bonds of marriage invariably results in the qualitative and quantitative impoverishment of the household. Children who are not raised in healthy households are undersocialized and become a significant socio-political liability.

6. Johannes Althusius recommendation regarding marriage should, on balance, be adopted:

> The husband communicates to his wife his name, family, reputation, station in life, and economic condition. He also provides her with guidance, legal protection, and defense against violence and injury. . . . Finally, he supplies her with all other necessities, such as management, solicitude, food, clothing. . . .
>
> The wife extends to her husband obedience, subjection, trust, compliance, services, support, aid, honor, reverence, modesty, and respect. She brings forth children for him, and nurses and trains them. She joins and consoles him in misery and calamity. She accommodates herself to his customs, and without his counsel and consent she does nothing. And thus she renders to her husband an agreeable and peaceful life. . . . There are also common advantages and responsibilities that are provided and communicated by both spouses, such as kindness, use of the body for avoiding harlotry and for procreating children, mutual

habitation, intimate and familiar companionship, mutual love, fidelity, patience, mutual service, communication of all goods and right (jus) . . . management of the family, administration of household duties, education of children in the true religion, protection against and liberation from perils, and mourning of the dead.[39]

7. Homosexuality cannot be constituted in the form of marriage, as marriage is, by nature, intended for the bonding of man and woman, husband and wife, as the foundation for the household (combining the objectives of preservation and improvement) and the fulfillment of the ritual of citizenship. Homosexual relations should not be viewed as "equal" with heterosexual relations as the former are *contra* nature and the latter congruent with the transcendental standard of nature. Two men cannot conceive a child (a potential "person" and therefore "citizen") and neither can two women. *Artificial* insemination in the case of unmarried individuals or homosexual partners must be forbidden. Adoption must only be permitted in the case of a married heterosexual couple.

III

In as much as the private associations of marriage and the household form the cornerstone of a free, self-governing polity, it is necessary that their arrangement be conducive to the preservation and perpetuation of the principles of responsibility and civility. For this reason, public policy should require that their structure be constituted in accordance with the standard of nature disclosed by reason.

This chapter has proposed this appropriate natural arrangement in this way providing a general framework for the institution of public philosophy or the role of reason in a constitutional order. The breakdown of the family is symptomatic of the crisis of public philosophy. Without healthy, vibrant families in which men and women dedicate their lives to their union and their children, civic virtue is impossible. Families are the microcosms in which public duty and citizenship are cultivated and born. Family life is national life writ large. It is within marriage and the household that we not only best preserve ourselves, but best improve ourselves. Marriage and family life naturally associate freedom with responsibility in the language of virtue and in the form of character. Michael Novak states the point well:

> In free societies, the language of virtue and character is indispensable—so indispensable as to be prosaic, indeed. For how can a people profess to be capable of self-government—of government of, by, and for the people—if they cannot govern their own passions? How can a people govern a whole society that cannot, each of them, govern themselves? In the free society, virtue is a sine qua non. Where there is no virtue, the free society perishes and the very idea of liberty becomes chimerical.[40]

It is by committing ourselves to our marriages and families, to union and citizenship, that we cultivate public virtue and become fully human. To live well in our households, we share in the wisdom of life and not only pursue happiness, but obtain it by fulfilling the principle of self-government. The institutions of marriage and the family are at the core of public policy in a constitutional order. The most important teachers in civil society are parents as they first instill in their children the principles by which we live: that we are all created equal, and that we are all, therefore, equally free (right) and equally responsible (reason). The constitution of public philosophy begins at home.

Chapter 9

Conclusion: The Constitution of Public Philosophy

. . . the most authoritative of the sciences . . . is manifestly the science of politics; for it is this that ordains which of the sciences are to exist in states, and what branches of knowledge the different classes of the citizens are to learn, and up to what point; and we observe that even the most highly esteemed of the faculties, such as strategy, domestic economy, oratory, are subordinate to the political science. Inasmuch then as the rest of the sciences are employed by this one, and as it moreover lays down laws as to what people shall do and what things they shall refrain from doing, the end of this science must include the ends of all the others. Therefore, the good of man must be the end of the science of politics.

Aristotle
Nicomachean Ethics

This analysis began with the stipulation that Western civilization is in crisis. The crisis of the West "consists in the West having become uncertain of its purpose."[1] Political science or philosophy was traditionally directed (in the Platonic-Aristotelian sense) toward the good of man in a way that tied the preservation and perfection of human nature with the purpose of political life.[2] The crisis of Western civilization is, therefore, a crisis of political science or philosophy, the public application of which is public philosophy. Western civilization has become estranged from the traditional science of politics, the exclusive enterprise dedicated toward human civilization. Western political life has become alienated from the life of reason and the pursuit of wisdom.

Now whereas it is indisputable that political philosophy cannot exist or flourish without the political, what has been neglected in our time is the great extent to which the political cannot exist or flourish without philosophy. The disparity between politics and philosophy is derivative of the Enlightenment and the governmental institutions which it produced. In the American case, constitutional forms were erected on the basis of freedom negatively understood in order to secure the basic rights of humanity. This constitutionalism has indeed effectively secured basic human rights, but has not informed the citizenry in a positive way regarding the duties or responsibilities of free living. The missing ingredient of the American new science of politics is an anti-pragmatic, contemplative component—political philosophy. The near absence of political philosophy in the United States has resulted in the politicization of American life as well as the politicization of American political science. American life needs political philosophy and in order for this need to be fulfilled, American political science must become more philosophical. Without a redirection in American political science, American political life will continue to atomize under the pressures of radical egalitarianism and individualism, the diseases of unqualified or excessive democratization, and American political science will increasingly wander pragmatically in superficiality and super-fluity under the guise of expertise.

To a large extent, the American crisis of an incomplete constitutionalism is symptomatic of the crisis of Western civilization. The independent force of public philosophy is in disrepair and civilization is at stake. The rejuvenation of political philosophy in the United States must be directed toward linking the purpose of constitutional life with the end of humanity, the good, or justice. American constitutionalism, with its protection of the rights of humanity equally before the rule law requires the informative, guiding interest of reason. The solution to the crisis of American constitutionalism and Western civilization is the constitution of public philosophy.

I

There are three basic questions inherent in the study of government and politics: 1) Why government?, 2) What kind?, and 3) Who should govern? These questions were addressed by the American framers. Their answer to the question of the necessity of government was rooted in a skeptical view of human nature. James Madison was eloquent and yet straightforward in asserting: "But what is government itself, but the greatest of all reflections on human nature? If men were angels, no government would be necessary."[3] The purpose of government from this perspective is predominantly one of controlling the effects of human nature by artificially creating institutions and mechanisms which prevent tyranny. The kind of government the framers prescribed was in light of this view of human nature, the rule of law (as opposed to tyranny or the rule of will). The law applies to all equally and is a product of popular sovereignty. It follows that the answer to the question of who should rule is the people, albeit indirectly in accordance with the republican principle of representation. The skeptical view of human nature which informed the American founding led to a general skepticism regarding the possibility of wise rule absent certain precautionary devices. This sober-minded approach to the establishment of a free political order was a marked advance in the science of politics, one which ought to be preserved.

It is, however, necessary to reflect upon these three questions further in order to provide a comprehensive response to each. While the American framers noted the negative, passionate, characteristics of human nature, their approach to the question of the fundamental purpose of government deviated from the transcendental standard of nature which comprehensively includes both humanity and the natural environment in one dialectically woven whole. Human beings are, "by nature," social or political beings. It is in their nature to live in a polity or society.[4] Indeed, human beings preserve themselves socially by way of heterosexual reproduction and improve themselves politically by the utilization of speech, the human expression of thought or reason. The basic purpose of government cannot therefore be exclusively the negative, legal, institutional regulation of passionate human behavior. The objective of government must also be positive, character forming, and moral. The law alone cannot accomplish this second purpose as it is expressly intended to be limited in range and scope. And yet, this objective, the education and nurturing of the members of the polity in the form of citizenship is nonetheless expedient.

The rule of law by written constitution, incorporating the principles of natural equality and right via the institutionalization of the separation of powers, checks and balances, federalism, and republican representation secures freedom by externally limiting government and the governed.[5] But this approach to the question of what kind of government is qualitatively best falls short of comprehending the degree to which citizens need positive direction concerning the internal regulation of themselves (i.e., self-government). Self-government is not automatic by nature and without a substantially self-governing citizenry, the rule of law collapses from the weight of lawlessness, incivility, unreason.

The constitution of a free and equal people (popular sovereignty) and the constitution of a government which secures the rights of that people (the rule of law) demands the constitution of public philosophy (the rule of reason) in order for the dialectic of freedom (negative and positive) to be complete. The American new science of politics, based as it was on Enlightenment rationality, created an almost self-sufficient instrument for governance. The Constitution has required little more than fine-tuning, or minor adjustments. However, the public sphere or domain which is not directly addressed by the law is in need of considerable maintenance. This is not to say that the law and the sphere of freedom or public privacy which it protects (the domain of social relations which is deemed to be outside the purview of the law) are separate and distinct entities, they are not. The law must support free, responsible living, and the public philosophy must support the rule of law. It is to say that the law, in and of itself, cannot provide the positive role of reason which free, responsible living requires. This role must be provided by American political science or philosophy. In a constitutional order, the people must rule themselves by law, and this form of rule (self-government) must of necessity be informed by the rule of the wise, by public philosophy.

II

Whereas constitutionalism qualifies or limits democracy, political philosophy qualifies constitutionalism. In what specific way then can political philosophy limit constitutional democracy and why is such a qualification necessary?

The regime which the American framers created secures the rights of humanity more effectively than any other. And yet, the principle strength of constitutionalism is also its core weakness. American political culture is fundamentally pragmatic, or anti-philosophical. Alexis de Tocqueville, a French aristocrat himself, observed the anti-aristocratic (democratic) tendencies of Americans and their way of life:

> I think that in no country in the civilized world is less attention paid to philosophy than in the United States . . . in most of the operations of the mind each American appeals only to the

> individual effort of his own understanding. . . . The practice of Americans leads their minds to other habits, to fixing the standard of their judgment in themselves alone . . . they readily conclude that everything in the world may be explained, and that nothing in it transcends the limits of the understanding. Thus they fall to denying what they cannot comprehend. . . . This disposition of mind soon leads them to condemn forms, which they regard as useless and inconvenient veils.[6]

American pragmatism is an impediment to the constitution of public philosophy. Americans distrust intellectual authority and are led to neglect theory. This tendency has had a profound impact upon American political science proper. Tocqueville perceived that Americans, as a result of the equality of their social condition, are addicted to practical science. In contrast, he pointed out that aristocracies often uphold philosophy (the pursuit of wisdom for its own sake), the effect of which is to "raise greatly the general pitch of society."[7] Tocqueville understood the extent to which Americans shun philosophy as a result of its aristocratic flavor, its exclusivity, its note of superiority. He feared that American civilization could perish as a direct result of this anti-philosophical disposition:

> If the light by which we are guided is ever extinguished, it will dwindle by degrees and expire of itself. By dint close adherence to mere applications, principles would be lost sight of; and when the principles were wholly forgotten, the methods derived from them would be ill pursued. New methods could no longer be invented, and men would continue, without intelligence and without art, to apply scientific processes no longer understood.[8]

Pragmatism is a uniquely American manner of thought and action which places thought in the service of action. Classical philosophy emphasized the opposite, it maintained the importance of contemplation, of thought before action. The origins of American society are rooted in Enlightenment rationality and democratic equality, neither of which can support the moral and intellectual condition of a free people. Only political philosophy can put forth those ideas which constitute the character of mind which is conducive to the maintenance of an American democratic republic.[9] This is the paradox confronting post-modern America. The polity is substantially anti-philosophical and is in dire need of political philosophy.

Another way of stating this problematic is as follows: constitutional democracy must have some transcendental source which gives it meaning and support. Constitutional democracy is not self-sufficient. In fact, there are tendencies in democratic times which serve to subvert constitutional democracy such as radical egalitarianism and individualism. These tendencies, when applied to the realm of political thought, serve to equalize, and therefore atomize and relativize the authority of contemplation, of ideas, of the forms necessary for the perpetuation of free, constitutional living. Constitutional democracy is need of aristocracy of a certain kind, an aristocracy of human excellence (as opposed to landed interests, property ownership, socio-economic classification, genealogy, etc.). Classically, human excellence was rooted in the life and cultivation of the mind. Constitutional democracy requires an aristocracy of political philosophy.

Without the guiding and moderating forces of reason, constitutional democracy becomes enveloped by mass culture which "is appropriated by the meanest capacities without any intellectual and moral effort whatsoever."[10] Mass culture eventually destroys constitutional democracy since it emancipates the passions while depreciating the intellectual and moral regulation of them. John Stuart Mill was speaking for his age when he asserted that "the only purpose for which power can be rightfully exercised over any member of a civilized community, against his will, is to prevent harm to others."[11] What is important to emphasize, however, is that his principle is fully contingent upon the qualification of civilization. Mill's conception of limited external government which is so popular in our time is entirely dependent upon the civility of the citizenry. And the civility of the people demands a certain kind of nurturing, the kind which can only be provided by education in reason, by political philosophy. Political philosophy plays an educational role in society which inculcates civility and responsibility in the citizenry, informing them in terms of the principles and virtues of self-government.

III

The great problematic which must now be confronted is one which Plato articulated in the *Republic*. If the best form of government is a regime ruled by the wise, by philosopher-kings, how can this social and political ordering of things be made practicable? Whereas the wise should rule, they 1) do not desire rule or power, and 2) the people do not desire them to rule. These conditions make the rule of wisdom extremely unlikely.

The contention of this research is that the rule of the wise can occur indirectly, it can be communicated educationally in the form of public philosophy. It is indeed the case that Americans are not particularly predisposed to have affection for forms, for political philosophy. And yet, it also clear that the Constitution expressly protects the right to reason, or the activity of political philosophy. In other words, the social condition of the United States is anti-philosophical but protects political philosophy simultaneously. There is a natural diversity in the faculties and capacities of citizens, the protection of which is the first object of constitutional government.[12] It follows that there will be a certain number of individuals who by their essential nature and training will possess and cultivate talents and virtue in such a way as to distinguish themselves from others. In a free society, a natural aristocracy of political philosophers can emerge, given the appropriate conditions. Thomas Jefferson contemplated the value of this natural aristocracy among men:

> The natural aristocracy I consider as the most precious gift *of nature*, for the instruction, the trusts, and government of society. And indeed, it would have been inconsistent *in creation* to have formed man for the social state, and not to have provided virtue and wisdom enough to manage the concerns of society. May we not even say, that that form of government is best, which provides the most effectually for a pure selection of these natural aristoi into the offices of government (emphasis added)?[13]

There is a direct relationship between securing justice and assuring that those individual citizens who are most just play a significant role in governance. For this reason, the Athenian Stranger in Plato's *Laws* provides for a Nocturnal Council of rulers who have distinguished themselves in human philosophic excellence, and who affix the standards of public virtue.[14] Note the words of the early American writing *The Preceptor*:

> The welfare, nay *the nature* of civil society requires, that there should be a subordination of order, or diversity of ranks and conditions in it; that certain men or orders of men be appointed to superintend and manage such affairs as concern the public safety and happiness (emphasis added).[15]

Thomas Jefferson also comprehended the importance of developing the reasoning faculties of our youth, of enlarging their minds, cultivating their morals, and instilling into them the precepts of virtue and order. He therefore understood that education generates habits of application, or order, and the love of virtue; and controls by the force of habit, any innate obliquities in our moral organization."[16] The habits which Jefferson believed to be the outcome of education, Alexis de Tocqueville considered to be "the various notions and opinions current among men and to the mass of those *ideas* which *constitute the character of mind*," and which comprise "the whole moral and intellectual condition of a people (emphasis added)."[17] There is a direct relationship between education and civic habituation or the inculcation of the public virtue necessary for free constitutional living. It is not simply the laws which govern a free people. The citizenry of a free society must, by means of a certain kind of education (in reason), develop the customs and traditions of civility. In the words of Tocqueville:

> I should say that physical circumstances are less efficient than the laws, and the laws infinitely less so than the customs of the people. I am convinced that the most advantageous situation and the best possible laws cannot maintain a constitution in spite of the customs of a country; . . . The importance of customs is a common truth to which study and experience incessantly direct our attention. . . . So seriously do I insist upon this head that, if I have hitherto failed in making the reader feel the important influence of the practical experience, the habits, the opinions, in short, of the customs of the Americans upon the maintenance of their institutions, I have failed in the principal object of my work.[18]

The development of a natural aristocracy of political philosophers creates and perpetuates the customs of responsible self-government in accordance with the principles of reason since the philosopher contributes to society by "doing his own work, by his own well-being, he contributes to the well-being of the city: philosophy has necessarily a humanizing or civilizing effect."[19] This natural aristocracy of political philosophy completes the equation of constitutionalism, of freedom and responsibility, of the rule of law and the rule of reason.

The instrument for the establishment of the indirect rule of the wise is the university, and within the university, political science. The American university has, true to Tocqueville's observations, become infatuated with modern Enlightenment science. And, this proclivity has effected American political science to the extent that "political studies suffer from over-emphasizing science while paying insufficient attention to the realm of morals, where men may be impelled to behave well and inspired to resist wrong-doing."[20] American political science has periodically embraced the notion that the primary purpose of the discipline is providing citizenship education. However, it has often forgotten that this objective provides a unifying force not only within American political science, but in constitutional society generally. "If not the promotion of good citizenship, what conceivable service could a political discipline render, except for tendering advice to wealthy clients?"[21] And of course, political science must defend itself before the public tribunal, it must demonstrate its social and political worth in order to be held in esteem.

IV

American political science can play a formative role in fulfilling the objectives of 1) education toward enlightened citizenship, 2) education toward enlightened statesmanship, and 3) education toward enlightened education. Indeed, there must be the establishment of an essential relationship between political science and the training of the citizenry at every level if public philosophy is to become actualized.

The schools and colleges serve a basic function of educating the citizenry in the United States not only in terms of reading, writing, and arithmetic, but in public virtue and citizenship. American political science is the discipline uniquely situated to guide character formation and citizen enlightenment. In order for the discipline to accomplish this goal, it would be particularly useful if Departments of American political philosophy were instituted at colleges and universities and a citizenship curriculum created for junior and senior high school students. These Departments would have as their primary goal the education of the citizenry in the principles of reasonable self-government. The national curriculum would need to consist of a series of courses in the Western tradition of political philosophy beginning with the Platonic dialogues and extending through the present; as well as a series of courses rooted in the American founding which would include the *Declaration of*

Independence, the *Federalist*, the *Constitution*, Locke's *Second Treatise of Government*, etc.[22] This combination of courses would sufficiently prepare citizens, and potential statesmen and educators in the intellectual-moral foundations of Western civilization as well as the institutional framework of constitutionalism and human rights. The standards of justice which these courses and great works would reveal and address form a natural-right tradition of Socratic assessment which serves as an independent standard for judging public affairs.[23]

In accordance with the natural right principles of the *Declaration of Independence*, Americans are literally born free and equal. Abraham Lincoln perceived that American citizenship is rooted in the creation of a new nation, "conceived in Liberty and dedicated to the proposition that all men are created equal."[24] From this perspective, "to be human is to be a citizen."[25] In other words, American citizenship must mean much more than what is given at birth by birth as the concept is inextricably tied to what it means to be fully human. And, the example *par excellence* of the qualitative combination of human excellence and excellent citizenship was the life of Socrates.[26] American citizenship must by definition and by nature be informed by political philosophy. The most fully human life is the examined life and those who live the examined life are the best citizens. "The highest form of justice is the preserve of those who have the greatest self-sufficiency which is humanly possible;" as self-governance is the art and craft of living reasonably, it is the life of the wise.[27]

For this reason, American political science must be rededicated to the disciplinary goal of civic education. This education in reason will moderate the democratic passions and elevate the habits of mind over matter, of self-discipline, by institutionalizing them in the form of custom. The traditions of civility (of reason) maintain and form "a true community . . . like the thread which holds the pieces of fabric together."[28] It is the tradition of reason or political philosophy which must form the public philosophy of American constitutionalism.

While the role of public philosophy is predominantly social, and not legal, legal support of public philosophy is required. This support can best come from the passage of national legislation which augments the XIV Amendment to the U.S. Constitution. Whereas "all persons born or naturalized in the United States and subject to the jurisdiction thereof, are citizens of the United states," national legislation should be passed which holds that "all citizens of the United States must be educated in a national curriculum of constitutional citizenship to be administered by Departments of American political philosophy." This legislation would ensure that citizens not only understand their constitutional rights, but their constitutional responsibilities as well. In addition, legislation should be passed which stipulates that "all citizens of the United States must complete a minimum of one year of national public service prior to the age of twenty-one" (assisting the poor and elderly, military service, environmental protection and conservation, youth programs such as the Boy Scouts, Girl Scouts, etc.).[29] This education in citizenship and public service would instruct citizens in the meaning and purpose of self-government within the context of the classical tradition of reason.

Alexander Hamilton maintained that the security of the rights of the people would be found in the original Constitution and therefore argued against the adoption of a Bill of Rights. He even believed that a Bill of Rights would be dangerous:

> But a minute detail of particular rights is certainly far less applicable to a Constitution like that under consideration, which is merely intended to regulate the general political interests of the nation, than to a constitution which has the regulation of every species of personal and private concerns. . . . They would contain various exceptions to powers not granted; and, on this very account, would afford colorable pretext to claim more than were granted. For why declare that things shall not be done which there is no power to do?[30]

Hamilton was referring to the fact that the Constitution was expressly intended to prevent tyranny by means of limited government. And, if government is to be limited, the written law must both limit and be limited. The rule of law must specifically limit rights as without this qualification, law can potentially be utilized to either circumvent or contravene its own principles by declaring rights where none exist "by nature."[31] And yet, if the Constitution is not intended to enumerate rights and is only meant to "regulate the general interests of the nation," what could possibly "regulate every species of personal and private concerns?" Hamilton alludes to the answer to this question in pointing out that a recognition of popular rights was already partially listed in several of the State bills of rights, which he believed "would sound much better in a treatise of ethics than in a constitution of government."[32]

Hamilton's remark points toward the solution of the debate between the Federalists and the Anti-Federalists, one which in various shapes and forms has persisted to the present. Granted, the Bill of Rights was adopted and is now, in all likelihood, here to stay. And yet, Hamilton was correct in fearing the dangers of a constitutional Bill of Rights as the post-modern American fixation upon rights to the exclusion of responsibilities has reached a near breaking-point.

The States have always assumed the responsibility of educating the nations citizenry, in families, communities, and schools. This should continue. There must, however, be a national recognition of the rights of citizenship which a Constitution secures. This has traditionally been inculcated by way of civic education in public "State" schools (national, constitutional education at the "State" level). There must also be a national, educational recognition of the duties, the formal obligations of citizenship which a Constitution requires. These two components of civic education in a constitutional order (of the rights and responsibilities of citizenship in terms of American Founding principles and classical philosophic directives mentioned above) must be formulated into a "treatise of ethics," into a public philosophy, not as part of the written law, but as a founding cornerstone which compliments it. The public philosophy completes the dialectic of free, constitutional living by guiding and directing the personal, but naturally social lives of Americans. The articulation and perpetuation of the public philosophy requires the indirect rule of political philosophy. In the United States, this indirect rule of reason must be made the preserve of American political science.

V

The Western tradition of political thought has produced a vast body of knowledge and wisdom. None of its precepts are more important than those elucidated in Plato's *Republic*: that justice is the end of government, that it is the same for individuals and the state, and that it is to found by way of reason, by means of political philosophy. There is a natural and undeniable correlation between justice and reason, between living-well and contemplation.

Whether the American twenty-first century will be blessed with a new birth of human excellence in civility or cursed by human ignorance in barbarism largely depends upon whether the absolute need for the indirect rule of wisdom based upon the transcendental standard of nature is recognized and acknowledged.[33] One of the most important political philosophers of the twentieth century openly wondered whether the United States still cherished the faith in which it was conceived, whether its people still held the truths of equality and the natural rights of life, liberty, and the pursuit of happiness to be self-evident.[34] It is here necessary to push this question even further, to exhaust it. Is this same nation sufficiently humble and thoughtful to pursue and understand truth proper? Is it willing to listen to reason? The future of constitutionalism, and therefore human freedom and justice, is intertwined with the fate of political philosophy. Whether political power will be joined with philosophical rule by the constitution of public philosophy is the question of our time. It is the question of all time, politically and philosophically speaking.

Notes

Chapter 1

1. Walter Lippmann, *The Public Philosophy* (New York, NY: Mentor Books, 1955), p. 19.
2. Jose' Ortega y Gasset, *The Revolt of the Masses* (New York, NY: W.W. Norton & Co., 1957), p. 16.
3. Allan Bloom, *The Closing of the American Mind* (New York, NY: Simon & Schuster, 1987).
4. Walter Lippmann, *The Public Philosophy*, p. 74.
5. Jose' Ortega y Gasset, *The Revolt of the Masses*, p. 73.
6. Leo Strauss, *What Is Political Philosophy?* (Chicago, IL: University of Chicago Press, 1959), pp. 11-12.
7. Allan Bloom, *Giants and Dwarfs: Essays 1960-1990* (New York, NY: Simon & Schuster, 1990).
8. Plato, *The Republic*, Benjamin Jowett, trans. (New York, NY: Vintage Books, 1984), Book VII.
9. See Leo Strauss, *Natural Right and History* (Chicago, IL: University of Chicago Press, 1953), pp. 1-9, 81-164.
10. Eric Voegelin, *The New Science of Politics* (Chicago, IL: University of Chicago Press, 1987), pp. 4, 27-28.
11. For an excellent examination of these two kinds of freedom see Giovanni Sartori, "Liberty and Law," in Kenneth S. Templeton, Jr., *The Politicization of Society* (Indianapolis, Indiana: Liberty Press, Inc., 1979), pp. 251-311.
12. See Aristotle, *The Politics*, T.J. Saunders, trans. (New York, NY: Penguin Books, 1981, Book III; and Giovanni Sartori, "Liberty and Law, it p. 263.
13. Alexander Hamilton, John Jay, and James Madison, *The Federalist* (Springfield, VA: Global Affairs Publishing Co., 1987), p. 28.
14. Leo Strauss, "Progress or Return," in Thomas L. Pangle, ed. *The Rebirth of Classical Political Rationalism* (Chicago, IL: University of Chicago Press, 1989), pp. 227-270.
15. In a society where the law protects freedom of conscience, religious differences invariably arise making a religious foundation and standard for society as a whole untenable.

16. Leo Strauss, *Natural Right and History*, p. 89.
17. See Thomas Jefferson, "The Declaration of Independence," in Robert C. Baron, *Soul of America: Documenting Our Past 1492-1974* (Golden, Colorado, Fulcrum, Inc., 1989), p. 45-48.
18. *Federalist #10* has been misinterpreted and misunderstood by American political scientists resulting in the proliferation of a pluralist interpretation of Madisonian democracy in the U.S. See for example, Robert A. Dahl, *A Preface to Democratic Theory* (Chicago, IL: University of Chicago Press, 1956); and a critique of Dahl's work by Harvey C. Mansfield, Jr., *America's Constitutional Soul* (Baltimore, MD: Johns Hopkins University Press, 1991), pp. 1-1 7.
19. See David M. Ricci, *The Tragedy of Political Science: Politics, Scholarship, and Democracy* (New Haven, CT: Yale University Press, 1984), p. 25.
20. See Herbert J. Storing, ed., *Essays on the Scientific Study of Politics* (New York, NY: Holt, Rinehart and Winston, 1962); George J. Graham, Jr. and George W. Carey, eds. *The Post-Behavioral Era: Perspectives on Political Science;* E. Robert Statham, Jr., *Between Inquiry and Advocacy: A Critique of the Pragmatic Foundations of Academic Public Policy* (Boone, NC: Parkway Publishers, 1995); and Theodore J. Lowi, "The State in Political Science: How We Became What We Study," *American Political Science Review* 86 (March 1992): pp. 1-7, for a sample of critiques of the state of the discipline of American political science.
21. Alexis de Tocqueville, *Democracy in America* (Vol. II) (New York, NY: Vintage Books, 1990), p. 3.
22. Donald W. Hanson, "The Education of Citizens: Reflections on the State of Political Science," *Polity* (Summer 1979), pp. 457-477.
23. Howard Slaatte, *Our Cultural Cancer And Its Cure* (Lanham, MD: University Press of America, 1995), p. 20.
24. Plato, *The Apology of Socrates*, Benjamin Jowett, trans. (Danbury, CT: Grolier Enterprises, 1980), p. 30.
25. Abraham Lincoln, "Address at Gettysburg," in Robert C. Baron, *Soul of America*, pp. 267.
26. Aristotle, *The Politics*, T.J. Saunders, trans., (New York, NY: Penguin Books, 1981), 1252a1.
27. Aristotle, *The Nicomachean Ethics*, J.A.K. Thomson, trans., (New York, NY: Penguin Books, 1976), 1177b33-1178a21.

Chapter 2

1. Louis Hartz, "The Liberal Tradition In America," in Ann G. Serow, W. Wayne Shannon, and Everett C. Ladd, eds., *The American Polity Reader* (New York: W.W. Norton & Company, 1990), pp. 14-20.
2. Alexis de Tocqueville, *Democracy in America* (Volume II) (New York: Vintage Classics, 1990), p. 3; and Rene Descartes, *Discourse on Method* (Indianapolis, Indiana: Hacket Publishing Company, 1980), p. 18.
3. Leo Strauss, "Political Philosophy and The Crisis of Our Time," in George J. Graham, Jr. and George W. Carey, eds., *The Post-Behavioral Era: Perspectives on Political Science* (New York: David McKay Company, Inc., 1972), pp. 217-242.
4. Leo Strauss, *What Is Political Philosophy?* (Chicago, IL: University of Chicago Press, 1959), pp. 27-55.
5. Alexander Hamilton, John Jay, and James Madison, *The Federalist*, ed. by M. L. Chadwick, (Springfield, VA: Global Affairs Publishing Co., 1987), (#51), p. 281.
6. David Hume, *An Enquiry Concerning Human Understanding* (Buffalo, NY: Prometheus Books, 1988), p. 20.
7. Ibid., pp. 77-78.
8. *Federalist* 10, p. 46.
9. *Federalist* 10, p. 46.
10. *Federalist* 10, p. 47.
11. *Federalist* 1, pp. 2-3.
12. *Federalist* 49, p. 276.
13. *Federalist* 51, p. 281.
14. Frank Fox and Clayne Pope, *American Heritage* (Denver, CO: Morton Publishing Co., 1985), p. 44.
15. Ralph Ketcham, *Framed for Posterity: The Enduring Philosophy of the Constitution* (Lawrence, Kansas: University of Kansas Press, 1993), pp. 30-31.
16. *Federalist* 51, p. 281.
17. Walter Berns, *Taking The Constitution Seriously* (Lanham, MD: Madison Books, 1987), pp. 64-121.
18. Robert C. Baron, *Soul of America: Documenting Our Past* (Boulder, CO: Fulcrum, Inc., 1989), p. 45.

19. Ketcham, *Framed for Posterity*, pp. 6-10; see also Martin Shapiro and R. Tresolini, *American Constitutional Law* (New York: Macmillan Publishing Co., 1983), pp. 8-14.
20. *Federalist* 1, p. 1.
21. See the "Preamble" to the United States Constitution in Baron, *Soul of America*, p. 87.
22. Shapiro and Tresolini, *American Constitutional Law*, p. 4.
23. Giovanni Sartori, "Liberty and Law," in Kenneth S. Templeton, Jr, ed., *The Politicization of Society* (Indianapolis, Indiana: Liberty Press, 1979), pp. 256-259.
24. Ibid., p. 262; see also Isaiah Berlin, *Four Essays on Liberty* (Oxford: Oxford University Press, 1969).
25. John Locke, *The Second Treatise of Government* (New York: Macmillan Publishing Co., 1986), pp. 15-17.
26. Ibid., pp. 16-17.
27. Ibid., p. 17.
28. *Federalist* 10, p. 49.
29. *Federalist* 10, pp. 46-47.
30. *Federalist* 10, p. 47.
31. *Federalist* 10, p. 47.
32. Berns, *Taking The Constitution Seriously*, pp. 160-161.
33. Ibid., p. 161.
34. *Federalist* 10, pp. 45-46.
35. *Federalist* 10, p. 47.
36. Berns, *Taking The Constitution Seriously*, p. 161.
37. Alexis de Tocqueville, *Democracy in America* (Volume 2), p. 28.
38. *Federalist* 10, p. 48.
39. Alexis de Tocqueville, *Democracy in America* (Volume 2), p. 96.
40. Ibid., p. 97; see also Eric Hoffer, *The True Believer* (New York: Mentor Books, 1951), p. 37.

Chapter 3

1. Alexander Hamilton, John Jay, and James Madison, *The Federalist*, ed. by M.L. Chadwick (Springfield, VA: Global Affairs Publishing, Co., 1987), (#51), p. 284.

2. Note the pervasive nature of the numerous evils/problems which are destroying American public and private life such as divorce, abortion, youth violence and crime, drug abuse, disrespect for authority—i.e., God, Law, Reason, educational disintegration, increased litigousness, governmental/institutional corruption, social atomization and technocratization, each of which can be ultimately traced to selfishness and pride. See for example, Russell Jacoby, *Dogmatic Wisdom* (New York: Anchor Books, Doubleday, 1994); William A Henry III, *In Defense of Elitism* (New York: Anchor Books, Doubleday, 1994); William J. Bennett, *The De-Valuing of America* (New York: Summit Books, 1992); Allan Bloom, *The Closing of the American Mind* (New York: Simon & Schuster, 1987).
3. Abraham Lincoln, "The Perpetuation of Our Political Institutions," in Robert A. Goldwin, ed., *On Civil Disobedience* (Chicago, IL: Rand McNally & Company, 1970), p. 2.
4. See George Carey, *In Defense of the Constitution* (Indianapolis, Indiana: Liberty Press, 1995), p. 6.
5. See Walter Lippmann, *The Public Philosophy* (New York: Mentor Books, 1955); Michael J. Sandel, *Democracy's Discontent: America in Search of a Public Philosophy* (Cambridge, MA: The Belknap Press of Harvard University Press, 1996); Jurgen Gebhardt, *Americanism: Revolutionary Order and Societal Self-Interpretation in the American Republic* (Baton Rouge, LA: Louisiana State University Press, 1993; and Leo Strauss, "The Crisis of Our Time," in George Graham, Jr. and George Carey, *The Post-behavioral Era: Perspectives on Political Science* (New York: David McKay Company, Inc., 1972).
6. Alexis de Tocqueville, *Democracy in America* (Volume 2), (New York: Vintage Classics, 1990), pp. 3-5.
7. Ibid., pp. 41-42.
8. See Leo Strauss, *What Is Political Philosophy?* (Chicago, IL: University of Chicago Press, 1959), pp. 9-27; and Leo Strauss, *Natural Right and History* (Chicago, IL: University of Chicago Press, 1965), pp. 120-124.
9. Aristotle, *The Politics* (New York: Penguin Books, 1987).
10. *Federalist* 51, p. 284.

11. *Federalist* 55, p. 304.
12. *Federalist* 57, p. 309.
13. *Federalist* 57, p. 309.
14. See Giovanni Sartori, "Liberty and Law," in Kenneth S. Templeton, Jr, ed., *The Politicization of Society* (Indianapolis, Indiana: Liberty Press, 1979), pp. 258-266.
15. Frank Fox and Clayne Pope, *American Heritage* (Denver, CO: Morton Publishing Co., 1985), p. 100; Lippmann, *The Public Philosophy*, p. 78.
16. Lippmann, *The Public Philosophy*, p. 80.
17. Eric Fromm, *Escape From Freedom* (New York: Avon Books, 1965), p. viii.
18. Ibid., pp. xiv, 126, 155.
19. Jose Ortega y Gasset, *The Revolt Of The Masses* (New York: W. W. Norton & Company, 1957), p. 18.
20. Ibid., p. 62; and Alexis de Tocqueville, *Democracy in America* (Volume 2), p. 4.
21. Ortega y Gasset, *The Revolt Of The Masses*, p. 73.
22. Lippmann, *The Public Philosophy*, p. 64; see also William MacDougal, *Social Psychology* (London: Methuen & Co., 1950), p. 38.
23. *Federalist* 10, p. 46.
24. Harvey Mansfield, Jr., *America's Constitutional Soul* (Baltimore, MD: Johns Hopkins University Press, 1991), pp. 193-208.
25. Alexis de Tocqueville, *Democracy in America* (Volume 2), pp. 252-253.
26. Ibid., p. 124.
27. See Carey, *In Defense of the Constitution*, pp. 46-49.
28. *Federalist* 10, p. 47.
29. *Federalist* 51, p. 283.
30. *Federalist* 51, p. 283.
31. *Federalist* 51, p. 283.
32. *Federalist* 49, p. 276.
33. *Federalist* 10, p. 46.
34. *Federalist* 10, p. 47.
35. Aristotle, *The Politics*, p. 54.

36. Theodore J. Lowi, *The End Of Liberalism: The Second Republic Of The United States* (New York: W. W. Norton & Co., 1979), pp. xi-22.
37. Mansfield, *America's Constitutional Soul*, p. 207.
38. William M. Sullivan, *Reconstructing Public Philosophy* (Berkeley, CA: University of California Press, 1982), p. 18.
39. Ibid., p. 19.
40. Jacques Ellul, "Politicization and Political Solutions," in Kenneth S. Templeton, Jr., ed., *The Politicization of Society* (Indianapolis, Indiana: Liberty Press, 1979), p. 225.
41. Eric Hoffer, *The True Believer* (New York: Mentor Books, 1951), pp. 130-133.
42. *Federalist* 51, p. 281.
43. Fromm, *Escape From Freedom*, pp. 155-180.
44. Friedrich Nietzsche, *Thus Spoke Zarathustra* (New York: Penguin Books, 1969), translated with Introduction by R.J. Hollingdale.
45. Ibid., p. 26.
46. Ortega y Gasset, *The Revolt Of The Masses*, p. 76.
47. Ibid., p. 72.
48. *Federalist* 10, p. 46.

Chapter 4

1. David M. Ricci, *The Tragedy of Political Science: Politics, Scholarship, and Democracy* (New Haven, CT: Yale University Press, 1984).; See E. Robert Statham, Jr., *Between Inquiry and Advocacy: A Critique of the Pragmatic Foundations of Academic Public Policy* (Boone, NC: Parkway Publishers, 1995) for a comprehensive examination of pragmatic rationality in American academic policy science.
2. See for example Herbert J. Storing, *Essays on the Scientific Study of Politics* (New York, NY: Holt, Rinehart, and Winston, 1962); Eric Voegelin, *The New Science of Politics* (Chicago, IL: University of Chicago Press, 1987); George J. Graham, Jr., and George W. Carey, *The Post-Behavioral Era* (New York, NY: David McKay Company, Inc., 1972); Sheldon S. Wolin, "Political Theory As A Vocation,"

American Political Science Review 63 (1969): 1062-1082; John Gunnell, "Deduction, Explanation, and Social Scientific Inquiry," *American Political Science Review* 63 (1969): 1233-1250; Paul F. Kress, "Against Epistemology: Apostate Musings," *The Journal of Politics* 41 (1979): 526-542; and Leo Strauss, *Natural Right and History* (Chicago, IL: University of Chicago Press, 1965).

3. See E. Robert Statham, Jr., "Carl Schmitt, Leo Strauss, and Heinrich Meier: A Dialogue Within the 'Hidden Dialogue'," *The Political Science Reviewer*, Volume XXVI, (1997); George W. Carey, *In Defense of the Constitution* (Indianapolis, IN: Liberty Press, 1995), pp. 6, 194.
4. Eric Voegelin, *The New Science of Politics*, pp. 4-5. Note that this critique of modern Western, and specifically American political science, is a generalization which cannot account for every part or aspect of the discipline. The generalization refers to an underlying tendency which has, and continues to predominate.
5. Leo Strauss, *Liberalism Ancient and Modern* (Ithaca, NY: Cornell University Press, 1989), p. 222.
6. See for example, Robert A. Dahl, *A Preface to Democratic Theory* (Chicago, IL: University of Chicago Press, 1956).
7. *The Federalist*, ed. Michael L. Chadwick (Springfield, VA: Global Affairs Publishing Co., 1987), p. 45.
8. See George W. Carey, "Political Science: A Split Personality," *Modern Age* 34 (1992).
9. Alexis de Tocqueville, *Democracy in America*, Volume II (New York, NY: Random House, Inc., 1990), pp. 41-47.
10. Ibid., p. 42.
11. Ibid., p. 43.
12. See for example, E. Robert Statham, Jr., *Between Inquiry and Advocacy*.
13. Voegelin, *The New Science of Politics*, p. 5.
14. For an account of the impoverished, fragmented nature of Political Theory or Philosophy within the discipline of political science see for example, John Gunnell, *Between Philosophy and Politics: The Alienation of Political Theory* (Amherst, MA: University of Massachusetts Press, 1986). See also Jerome J. Hanus, "Political Science: All Dressed Up and Nowhere to Go," *The Political Science Reviewer* XXV (1996): 4373.

15. Theodore Lowi, "The State in Political Science: How We Became What We Study," *American Political Science Review* 86 (1992): 1-7.
16. Voegelin, *The New Science of Politics*, p. 12.
17. Carey, "Political Science: A Split Personality," p. 103.
18. See Leo Strauss, *What Is Political Philosophy?* (Chicago, IL: University of Chicago Press, 1959), pp. 9-55; Plato, *The Republic*, Jowett Translation (New York, NY: Random House, Inc., 1985), Book VII, pp. 253-291.
19. Statham, *Between Inquiry and Advocacy*, p. 69.
20. See John Dewey, *Experience and Nature* (New York, NY: Dover Publications, 1958), p. 428.
21. See for example William M. Sullivan, *Reconstructing Public Philosophy* (Berkeley, CA: University of California Press, 1982), pp. 158-180; Harvey Mansfield, Jr., *America's Constitutional Soul* (Baltimore, MD: Johns Hopkins University Press, 1991), p. 139.
22. Theodore Lowi, *The End of Liberalism: The Second Republic of the United States* (New York, NY: W.W. Norton & Company, 1979), p. 22.
23. *The Federalist*, p. 47.
24. Lowi, *The End of Liberalism*, pp. 58-59.
25. E. E. Schattschneider, *The SemiSovereign People* (Hinsdale, IL: The Dryden Press, 1975), p. v.
26. Ibid., p. 138.
27. Strauss, *Liberalism Ancient and Modern*, p. 219.
28. Aristotle, *The Politics*, translated by T. A. Sinclair (New York, NY: Penguin Books, 1987), p. 54.
29. *The Federalist*, p. 47.
30. Mansfield, *America's Constitutional Soul*, pp. 190-191.
31. *The Federalist*, p. 46.
32. Ibid., p. 45.
33. Sheldon S. Wolin, "Max Weber: Legitimation, Method, and the Politics of Theory," *Political Theory* 9 (1981) pp. 406, 418.
34. Statham, "Carl Schmitt, Leo Strauss, and Heinrich Meier: A Dialogue Within the 'Hidden Dialogue'."
35. Ibid.
36. *The Federalist*, p. 283.
37. Ibid., p. 283.
38. Ibid., p. 283.

39. Ibid., p. 283.
40. Ibid., p. 301.
41. Ibid., p. 2.
42. Ibid., p. 309.
43. Ibid. p. 79.
44. See David Hume, *An Enquiry Concerning Human Understanding* (Buffalo, NY: Prometheus Books, 1988).
45. *The Federalist*, pp. 281, 276.
46. Leo Strauss, *Natural Right and History*, p. 314.
47. See Statham, "Carl Schmitt, Leo Strauss, and Heinrich Meier: A Dialogue Within The 'Hidden Dialogue'."
48. Leo Strauss, "Political Philosophy and the Crisis of Our Time," in eds. George J. Graham, Jr., and George W. Carey, *The Post-Behavioral Era* (New York, NY: David McKay Company, Inc., 1972), p. 239.
49. Ibid., p. 239.
50. Ibid., p. 242.
51. Mansfield, *America's Constitutional Soul*, p. 207.
52. Voegelin, *The New Science of Politics*, p. 27.
53. Ibid., p. 27.
54. Ibid., p. 27.
55. Ibid., p. 27.
56. Ibid., p. 158.
57. Ibid., p. 167.
58. Ibid., p. 179.
59. Hume, *An Enquiry Concerning Human Understanding*, p. 88.
60. Statham, "Carl Schmitt, Leo Strauss, and Heinrich Meier: A Dialogue Within The 'Hidden Dialogue'."
61. Thomas Hobbes, *Leviathan* (Great Britain: William Collins & Sons, 1983), p. 145.
62. Thomas Hobbes, *Leviathan*, ed. Michael Oakeshott (Blackstone ed.; oxford, s.a.), Introduction, p. 64.
63. Voegelin, *The New Science of Politics*, p. 180.
64. Statham, "Carl Schmitt, Leo Strauss, and Heinrich Meier: A Dialogue Within The 'Hidden Dialogue'."
65. Strauss, "Political Philosophy and the Crisis of Our Time," p. 222.

66. Carl Schmitt, *The Concept of the Political*, trans. by George Schwab, (Chicago, IL: University of Chicago Press, 1996).
67. Statham, "Carl Schmitt, Leo Strauss, and Heinrich Meier: A Dialogue Within The 'Hidden Dialogue'."
68. Voegelin, *The New Science of Politics*, p. 180.
69. Eric Fromm, *Escape From Freedom* (New York, NY: Avon Books, 1965), p. 155.
70. Sullivan, *Reconstructing Public Philosophy*, p. 12.
71. Frank W. Fox and Clayne L. Pope, *American Heritage* (Denver, CO: Morton Publishing Co., 1985), p. 40; See also Cass Sunstein, *The Partial Constitution* (Cambridge, MA: Harvard University Press, 1993), pp. 17-27.
72. Sullivan, *Reconstructing Public Philosophy*, p. 1-22.
73. *The Federalist*, p. 49.
74. *The Federalist*, p. 48. Note that the protection of the basic rights of individuals and the security of the public good are the primary object of constitutional government according to Madison.

Chapter 5

1. Niccolo Machiavelli, *The Prince*, translated by George Bull (New York, NY: Penguin Books, 1961), pp. 90-91.
2. Bertrand Russell, *Skeptical Essays* (London: Unwin Hyman Ltd., 1988), p. 43.
3. Leo Strauss, *What Is Political Philosophy?* (Chicago, IL: University of Chicago Press, 1959), p. 17.
4. Plato, *The Republic*, Jowett Translation (New York, NY: Vintage Books, 1984), Book VII.
5. Ibid., Book I.
6. Allan Bloom, *The Closing of the American Mind* (New York, NY: Simon and Schuster, 1987), pp. 25-28.
7. Leo Strauss, *On Tyranny*, eds. Victor Gourevitch and Michael S. Roth (New York, NY: The Free Press, 1991), p. 208.
8. Ibid., pp. 209-210.
9. See C.D.C. Reeve, *Philosopher-Kings: The Argument of Plato's Republic* (Princeton, NJ: Princeton University Press, 1988), pp. 140-143.

10. Leo Strauss, *On Tyranny*, p. 201.
11. David Hume, *An Enquiry Concerning Human Understanding* (Buffalo, NY: Prometheus Books, 1988), pp. 20, 77-78.
12. Plato, *The Republic*, pp. 163-165.
13. Ibid., pp. 159-166.
14. See Leo Strauss, "Political Philosophy and the Crisis of our Time," in eds. George J. Graham, Jr. and George W. Carey, *The Post-Behavioral Era: Perspectives on Political Science* (New York, NY: David McKay, Company, Inc., 1972), pp. 238-239; and Harvey Mansfield, *America's Constitutional Soul* (Baltimore, MD: The Johns Hopkins University Press, 1991), p. 207.
15. See Henry D. Thoreau, *Walden and On the Duty of Civil Disobedience* (New York, NY: MacMillan Publishing Co., 1962); and Herbert Hoover, "The Philosophy of Rugged Individualism," in Robert C Baron, ed., *Soul of America: Documenting Our Past 1492-1974* (Golden, CO: Fulcrum, Inc., 1989), pp. 334-338.
16. See Walter Lippmann, *The Public Philosophy* (New York, NY: Mentor Books, 1955).
17. Plato, *The Republic*, pp. 159-345.
18. Leo Strauss, *Natural Right and History* (Chicago, IL: University of Chicago Press, 1953), pp. 81-119.
19. Note lifestyles in regard to sexual orientation. See for example, Mark Blasius, "An Ethos of Lesbian and Gay Existence," *Political Theory* Vol. 20, No. 4 (November 1992), pp. 642-671.
20. Alexis de Tocqueville, *Democracy in America* (Vol. II) (New York, NY: Vintage Books, 1990), p. 97.
21. Bertrand Russell, *Autobiography* (London: Unwin Hyman Ltd., 1987), pp. 459-504.
22. Plato, *The Apology of Socrates* (Danbury, CT: Grolier Enterprises Corporation, 1980), p. 26.
23. See C.D.C. Reeve, *Philosopher-Kings: The Argument of Plato's Republic*, pp. 170-231 for an excellent account of the practicability of philosophic rule.
24. Ibid., p. 252.
25. Ibid., p. 50.
26. Ibid., p. 232.

27. See, for example, the 1st Amendment to the United States Constitution which protects freedom of speech. Speech, if it proceeds from deliberation, is a product of reason as opposed to the expression of passionate opinion.
28. Leo Strauss, "Political Philosophy and the Crisis of Our Time," pp. 222-223.
29. E. Robert Statham, Jr., "Carl Schmitt, Leo Strauss, and Heinrich Meier: A Dialogue Within the 'Hidden Dialogue'."
30. Aristotle, *The Politics* (New York, NY: Penguin Books, 1987), (1252a1).
31. *The Federalist*, ed. Michael L. Chadwick (Springfield, VA: Global Affairs Publishing Co., 1987), pp. 46-47.
32. Leo Strauss, *Liberalism Ancient and Modern* (Ithaca, NY: Cornell University Press, 1968), p. 16; *The Federalist #*'s: 10, 35, 36, 55, 57, 62, 68.
33. Robert Brown, *Classical Political Theories: From Plato to Marx* (New York, NY: MacMillan Publishing Company, 1990), p. 103.
34. Leo Strauss, *Liberalism Ancient and Modern*, p. 15.
35. E. Robert Statham, Jr., "Carl Schmitt, Leo Strauss, and Heinrich Meier: A Dialogue Within 'The Hidden Dialogue'."
36. Alexis de Tocqueville, *Democracy in America* (Vol. iI), pp. 10, 261.
37. *The Federalist*, p. 283.
38. Note Alexis de Tocqueville's concern that mass democracy lacks important elements of aristocratic excellence which give society refinement. See particularly Volume II of *Democracy in America* where this point pervades the entire work.

Chapter 6

1. Walter Lippmann, *The Public Philosophy* (New York, NY: Mentor Books, 1955), p. 79.
2. Ibid., p. 81.
3. See Leo Strauss, "An Epilogue" in ed. Herbert J. Storing, *Essays on the Scientific Study of Politics* (New York, NY: Holt, Rinehart and Winston, 1962), pp. 305-327. See also David Miller, ed., *Popper Selections* (Princeton, NJ: Princeton University Press, 1985), pp. 143-151.

4. See Cass R. Sunstein, *The Partial Constitution* (Cambridge, MA: Harvard University Press, 1993); See also Christopher Wolfe, *The Rise of Modern Judicial Review* (Lanham, MD: Rowman & Littlefield Publishers, Inc., 1994).
5. See Dino Bigongiari, ed., *The Political Ideas of St. Thomas Aquinas* (New York, NY: Hafner Press, 1953); and St. Augustine, *The City of God*, translated by Henry Bettenson (New York, NY: Penguin Books, 1984).
6. Note, for example, that the Church of Jesus Christ of Latter Day Saints (The Mormons) holds as doctrine that the U.S. Constitution is a divinely inspired document (See *Doctrine And Covenants* (Salt Lake City, UT: LDS Church, 1981), 101: 77-80). This is certainly related to the degree to which the Constitution of the United States protects freedom of religion, or conscience.
7. Many public policy issues touch upon matters of conscience and religious belief which cannot be confined to the private sphere (such as abortion, etc.).
8. Note the extent to which public policy debates are seemingly never-ending due to the positivistic-pluralistic-relativistic Vs. absolutist-religious polarity.
9. Richard Rorty, *Objectivity, Relativism, and Truth* (Cambridge: Cambridge University Press, 1991), pp. 23-24.
10. Ibid., p. 29.
11. Mark Blasius, "An Ethos of Lesbian and Gay Existence," *Political Theory* Vol. 20, No. 4 (November 1992), p. 642.
12. Ibid., p. 666. See for a counter-example E. Robert Statham, Jr, "Political Philosophy as Political Action: A Response to Mark Blasius," *Political Theory* Vol. 23, No. 3 (August 1995), pp. 517-519.
13. Leo Strauss, "An Epilogue," in ed. Herbert J. Storing, *Essays on the Scientific Study of Politics* (New York, NY: Holt, Rinehart and Winston, 1962).
14. Carl Schmitt, *Political Theology* (Cambridge, MA: The MIT Press, 1985), p. 66; See also, Carl Schmitt, *The Crisis of Parliamentary Democracy* (Cambridge, MA: MIT Press, 1985).
15. See William E. Scheuerman, "Carl Schmitt's Critique of Liberal Constitutionalism," *The Review of Politics* 58 (Spring 1996), pp. 314-315.

16. Statham, "Carl Schmitt, Leo Strauss, and Heinrich Meier: A Dialogue Within 'The Hidden Dialogue'."
17. Schmitt, *Political Theology*, p. 59.
18. Carl Schmitt, *The Concept of the Political* (New Brunswick, NJ: Rutgers University Press, 1976), p. 53; See also Giovanni Sartori, "The Essence of the Political in Carl Schmitt," *Journal of Theoretical Politics* 1:1 (January, 1989), pp. 69-71.
19. Note, for example, the pro-choice political activism which led to the Federal Judiciary sanctioning abortion (an extreme) and the recent pro-life activism which advocates the murder of medical doctors and assistants who perform abortions (a counter-extreme): Here the left meets the right in passionate conflict where reason is absent.
20. Leo Strauss, "Progress or Return?," in Thomas L. Pangle, ed., *The Rebirth of Classical Political Rationalism* (Chicago, IL: University of Chicaqo Press, 1989), p. 270.
21. Ibid., pp. 227-270.
22. Leo Strauss, *Jerusalem and Athens: Some Preliminary Reflections* (New York, NY: The City College Papers #6, 1967), pp. 3-28.
23. Strauss, "Progress or Return?," p. 270.
24. Alexis de Tocqueville, *Democracy in America* (Vol. II) (New York, NY: Random House, Inc., 1990), pp. 20-28, 143-151.
25. Ibid.; See also Sigmund Freud, *The Future of an Ilusion* (New York, NY: W.W. Norton & Co., 1961).
26. See Andrew A. Tadie and Michael H. Macdonald, *The Permanent Things* (Cambridge, UK: William B. Eerdmans Publishing Company, 1995).
27. Leo Strauss, *Natural Right and History* (Chicago, IL: University of Chicago Press, 1953), p. 314.
28. Statham, "Carl Schmitt, Leo Strauss, and Heinrich Meier: A Dialogue Within 'The Hidden Dialogue'."
29. Rene Descartes, *Discourse on Method* (Indianapolis, IN: Hackett Publishing Co., 1980), p. 18.
30. E. Robert Statham, Jr., "Nuclear Waste Disposal in Micronesia: A Cross-Cultural Analysis," *Asian Culture* Vol. XXIV, No. 2 (Summer 1996), pp. 1-19.
31. William Barrett, *Death of the Soul: From Descartes to the Computer* (New York, NY: Doubleday Publishing Co., 1986), P. 18.

32. E. Robert Statham, Jr., "Micronesian Navigational Philosophy and the Relationship Between Humanity and Nature: Etak/Itang—Where East Instructs West," *Asian Culture* Vol. XXV, No. 3 (November 1997), pp. 1-16.
33. Plato, *The Apology of Socrates*, Jowett translation (Grolier Enterprises Corp., 1980).
34. Strauss, *Natural Right and History*, p. 123.
35. Statham, "Micronesian Navigational Philosophy and the Relationship Between Humanity and Nature: Etak/Itanq—Where East Instructs West."
36. Strauss, *Natural Right and History*, p. 127.
37. Jose Ortega y Gasset, *What Is Philosophy?* (New York, NY: W.W. Norton & Co., 1960), p. 74.
38. Jacques Ellul, *The Technological Society* (New York, NY: Vintage Books, 1964), p. 29.
39. Bertrand Russell, "The Value of Philosophy" in *Problems of Philosophy* (London: Oxford University Press, 1912).
40. Karl Jaspers, *Origin and Goal of History* (1953), p. 271, as cited in Walter Lippmann, *The Public Philosophy* (New York, NY: Mentor Books, 1955), p. 105.
41. Lippmann, *The Public Philosophy*, pp. 106-107.
42. Ibid., p. 107.
43. Ibid., p. 107.
44. Ibid., p. 116.
45. Ibid., p. 135.
46. Eric Voegelin, *The New Science of Politics* (Chicago, IL: University of Chicago Press, 1952), pp. 61-62.
47. Cicero, *Republic*, trans. C.W. Keyes (Cambridge, MA: Harvard University Press, 1928), Book III, p. 33.
48. Plato, *The Laws*, trans. by A.E. Taylor (London, UK: J.M. Dent & Son's, 1960), p. 363 (966-967).
49. Ibid., pp.xvi-xvii.
50. Leo Strauss, *The City and Man* (Chicago, IL: Rand McNally & Co., 1964), p. 16.; See also Plato, *The Laws*, Book X.
51. Strauss, *The City and Man*, p. 16.
52. Cicero, *The Laws*, trans. C.W. Keyes (Cambridge, MA: Harvard University Press, 1928), Book I, 29-34, 47.

53. Hamilton, Jay, and Madison, *The Federalist*, Michael L. Chadwick ed. (Springfield, VA: Global Affairs Publishing Co., 1987), P. 1.
54. Plato, *The Republic*, Jowett trans. (Random House, 1984), Book IV.
55. C.D.C. Reeve, *Philosopher-Kings: The Argument of Plato's Republic* (Princeton, NJ: Princeton University Press, 1988), p. 205.
56. See for example William M. Sullivan, *Reconstructing Public Philosophy* (Berkeley, CA: University of California Press, 1982); and Michael J. Sandel, *Democracy's Discontent: America in Search of a Public Philosophy* (Cambridge, MA: The Belknap Press of Harvard University Press, 1996).
57. Lippmann, *The Public Philosophy*, pp. 96-98.
58. Cited in Herbert W. Schneider, *A History of American Philosophy* (1946), p. 517.
59. Leo Strauss, *The City and Man*, pp. 21-22.

Chapter 7

1. Bertrand Russell, *Unpopular Essays* (New York, NY: Simon and Schuster, 1950), p. 3.
2. Aristotle, *The Politics*, trans. by T.A. Sinclair (New York, NY: Penguin Books, 1962), p. 59 (1253aI).
3. Leo Strauss, "Political Philosophy and the Crisis of our Time," in eds. George J. Graham, Jr. and George W. Carey, *The Post-Behavioral Era: Perspectives on Political Science* (New York, NY: David McKay Company, Inc., 1972), p. 218.
4. See, for example, J.G.A. Pocock, *The Machiavellian Moment* (Princeton, NJ: Princeton University Press, 1975).
5. Wilfred M. McClay, "Communitarianism and the Federal Idea," *The Intercollegiate Review* Vol. 32, No. 2 (Spring 1997); See also Richard C. Sinopoli, *The Foundations of American Citizenship: Liberalism, The Constitution, And Civic Virtue* (Oxford, UK: Oxford University Press, 1992); and Felix Morley, *Freedom and Federalism* (Indianapolis, Indiana: Liberty Press, 1981).
6. Wilfred M. McClay, "Communitarianism and the Federal Idea," p. 39.
7. See Ralph Ketcham ed., *The Anti-Federalist Papers* (New York, NY: Mentor Books, 1986).

8. Herbert J. Storing, *What the Anti-Federalists Were For: The Political Thought of the Opponents of the Constitution* (Chicago, IL: University of Chicago Press, 1981), pp. 8-21.
9. David Popenoe, "The Family Condition of America: Cultural Change and Public Policy," in eds. Henry J. Aaron, Thomas E. Mann, and Timothy Taylor, *Values and Public Policy* (Washington, D.C.: The Brookings Institution, 1994), p. 86.
10. Note the extent to which it has become popular in the academy and media to deconstruct American history as well as noble statesmen and folk heroes. This is a pernicious and almost unexplainable form of intellectual sophistry that is seriously harming the American "Idea", and therefore American ideals.
11. Robert C. Baron, *The Soul of America: Documenting Our Past 1492-1974* (Golden, CO: Fulcrum, Inc., 1989), "The Declaration of Independence,", pp. 45-48.
12. Strauss, "Political Philosophy and the Crisis of Our Time," p. 239.
13. Ibid., p. 242.
14. Reinhold Niebuhr, *Moral Man and Immoral Society* (New York, NY: Charles Scribner's Sons, 1960), pp. xvi, xx.
15. Ibid., pp. xxiv, 32.
16. See James W. Ceaser, *Liberal Democracy & Political Science* (Baltimore, MD: Johns Hopkins University Press, 1990). Ceasar rightly suggests that political science must play a prominent role in maintaining constitutional democracy through civic education; See also Stewart Umphrey, *Zetetic Skepticism* (Wakefield, NH: Hollowbrook Publishing Inc., 1990), pp. 322-323. Umphrey concludes that Socratic philosophy (which forms the core of political philosophy) is the qualitatively best civilizing and humanizing influence available to us.
17. Harvey Mansfield, *America's Constitutional Soul* (Baltimore, MD: Johns Hopkins University Press, 1991), p. 217.
18. Ibid., pp. 201-202; See also Robert P. George, *Making Men Moral: Civil Liberties and Public Morality* (oxford, UK: Clarendon Press, 1993); and Aristotle, *The Politics*, trans. by T.A. Sinclair (New York, NY: Penguin Books, 1962), (1275b27-39).
19. Leo Strauss, *Liberalism Ancient and Modern* (Ithaca, NY: Cornell University Press, 1968), p. 5.

20. Paul Barry Clarke, *Citizenship* (London, UK: Pluto Press, 1994), p. 4.
21. Ibid., p. 7.
22. Plato, *Crito* (Danbury, CT: Grolier Enterprises Corp., 1980), pp. 31-44.
23. Plato, *The Apology of Socrates* (Danbury, CT: Grolier Enterprises Corp., 1980), pp. 26-30.
24. Ibid., p. 30.
25. Clarke, *Citizenship*, p. 21.
26. Alexis de Tocqueville, *Democracy in America* (Vol. II) (Random House, Inc., 1990), p. 41.
27. Bertrand Russell, *Skeptical Essays* (London, UK: Unwin Hyman Ltd., 1977), pp. 41-42.
28. James Q. Wilson, "Culture, Incentives, and the Underclass," in eds. Henry J. Aaron, Thomas E. Mann, and Timothy Taylor, *Values and Public Policy* (Washington, DC: The Brookings Institution, 1994), pp. 71-72.
29. Thomas L. Pangle, *The Ennobling of Democracy: The Challenge of the Postmodern Age* (Baltimore, MD: Johns Hopkins University Press, 1992), p. 168.
30. William J. Bennett ed., *The Book of Virtues: A Treasury of Great Moral Stories* (New York, NY: Simon & Schuster, 1993); and William J. Bennett ed., *The Moral Compass: Stories For Life's Journey* (New York, NY: Simon & Schuster, 1995).
31. William J. Bennett, *The De-Valuing of America: The Fight for Our Culture and Our Children* (New York, NY: Summit Books, 1992), p. 35.
32. David Hume, *An Enquiry Concerning the Principles of Morals*, ed. by J.B. Schneewind (Indianapolis, IN: Hackett Publishing Co., 1988), pp. 82-88.
33. Hadley Arkes, *First Things: An Inquiry Into the First Principles of Morals and Justice* (Princeton, NJ: Princeton University Press, 1986), p. 21.
34. Leo Strauss, *Natural Right and History* (Chicago, IL: University of Chicago Press, 1953), p. 127.
35. Plato, *The Republic*, Jowett trans. (New York: Random House Inc., 1984), p. 147, (433).

36. Clarke, *Citizenship*, p. 29.
37. Stephen Bertman (USIC Educational Foundation, 1990) cited in Anthony Harrigan, "A Lost Civilization," *Modern Age* Vol. 35, No. 1, p. 5.
38. Harrigan, "A Lost Civilization," pp. 6-7.
39. William A. Henry III, *In Defense of Elitism* (New York, NY: Anchor Books Doubleday, 1994), p. 35.
40. Bennett, *The De-Valuing of America*, p. 52.
41. The two prevalent tendencies in the American academy at present are neo-positivism and post-modern existentialism. The former holds the distinction between facts and values while the latter claims that all value is subjective and therefore relative.
42. *The Pacific Daily News*, July 20, 1997, p. 15. "The not-so-brand-new sound of rebellion and individualism—sizzling human flesh."
43. Allan Bloom, *Giants and Dwarfs: Essays 1960-1990* (New York, NY: Simon & Schuster, 1990), p. 387.
44. Strauss, *Natural Right and History*, pp. 145-146.
45. Ibid., pp. 135-136.
46. Abraham Lincoln, "The Perpetuation of Our Political Institutions," in Robert A. Goldwin ed., *On Civil Disobedience: American Essays, Old and New* (Chicago, IL: Rand McNally & Co., 1968), pp. 4-6.
47. Ibid., pp. 4-6.
48. Ibid., pp. 8-9; and Abraham Lincoln, "Address at Gettysburg," in Baron, *The Soul of America*, p. 267.

Chapter 8

1. See E. Robert Statham, Jr. "Micronesian Navigational Philosophy and the Relationship Between Humanity and Nature: Etak/Itang—Where East Instructs West," *Asian Culture* Vol. XXV, No. 3 (November 1997), pp. 1-16.
2. E.F. Schumacher, *Small Is Beautiful: Economics as if People Mattered* (New York, NY: Harper & Row Publishers, 1973), 14.
3. William Barrett, *Death of the Soul: From Descartes to the Computer* (New York, NY: Doubleday, 1986), p. 18.
4. Statham, Jr., "Micronesian Navigational Philosophy and the Relationship Between Humanity and Nature."

5. Hadley Arkes, *First Things: An Inquiry Into the First Principles of Morals and Justice* (Princeton, NJ: Princeton University Press, 1986), p. 21.
6. Louis Hartz, "The Liberal Tradition in America," in Ann G. Serow, W. Wayne Shannon, and Everett C. Ladd, eds., *The American Polity Reader* (New York, NY: W.W. Norton & Company, 1990), pp. 14-20.
7. Alexis de Tocqueville, *Democracy in America* (Vol. I) (New York, NY: Vintage Books, 1990), pp. 254-270.
8. Ibid., (Vol. II), pp. 3-7.
9. Aristotle, *The Politics*, trans. by T.A. Sinclair (New York, NY: Penguin Books, 1987), Book I.
10. Ibid., 1253aI.
11. Ibid., 1280a7.
12. James Fitzjames Stephen, *Liberty*, *Equality*, *Fraternity*, Stuart D. Warner, ed., (Indianapolis, Indiana: Liberty Fund, Inc., 1993), p. 153.
13. Alan Carlson, "Strengthening the Bonds of Civil Society," in Don E. Eberly, ed., *Building a Community of Citizens: Civil Society in the 21st Century* (Lanham, MD: University Press of America, 1994), pp. 294-295.
14. Aristotle, *The Politics*, 1252b27.
15. Ibid., 1253a7.
16. Ibid., 1253a18.
17. Ibid., 1253a7-1253a29.
18. Ibid., 1253a29.
19. Aristotle, *The Ethics*, trans. by J.A.K. Thomson (New York, NY: Penguin Books, 1976), 1177b13-1178a21.
20. Charles R. Kesler, "Character, Citizenship, and Consti-tutional Origins," in Don E. Eberly, ed., *The Content of America's Character: Recovering Civic Virtue* (Lanham, MD: Madison Books, 1995), p. 99.
21. James D. Sellmann, "Achieving Person Through Ritual," *Asian Culture* Vol. XXV, No. 2 (Summer, 1997), p. 1.
22. Eliot Deutsch, *Personhood*, *Creativity*, *and Freedom* (Honolulu, Hawaii: University of Hawaii Press, 1982), pp. 17-18, 114.

23. James D. Sellmann, pp. 2-7.
24. Charles R. Kesler, p. 103.
25. Ibid., p. 105.
26. Russell Kirk, "The Revitalized College: A Model," in Anne H. Burleigh, ed., *Education in a Free Society* (Indianapolis, Indiana: Liberty Press, 1978), p. 140.
27. Plato, *The Laws*, trans. by A.E. Taylor (London, U.K.: Everyman's Library, 1969), Book I.
28. Plato, *The Apology of Socrates*, trans. by B. Jowett (Danbury, CT: Grolier Enterprises Corp., 1980), p. 30.
29. Harvey C. Mansfield, Jr., *America's Constitutional Soul* (Baltimore, MD: Johns Hopkins University Press, 1991), p. 201.
30. Barbara D. Whitehead and David G. Blankenhorn, "Man, Woman and Family: Difference and Dependency in the American Conversation," in Don E. Eberly, ed., *Building a Community of Citizens: Civil Society in the 21st Century*, p. 216.
31. Plato, *The Laws*, 793, p. 176.
32. Johannes Althusius, *Politica*, Frederick S. Carney, ed., (Indianapolis, Indiana: Liberty Fund, Inc., 1995), p. 31.
33. Wade F. Horn, "Character and Family," in Don E. Eberly, ed., The Content of America's Character: Recovering Civic Virtue, pp. 80-81.
34. See Dino Bigongiari, Ed., *The Political Ideas of St. Thomas Aquinas* (New York, NY: Hafner Press, 1953).
35. Hadley Arkes, *First Things*, p. 162.
36. Barbara D. Whitehead and David G. Blankenhorn, "Man, Woman and Family," p. 216. The authors recommend that "no fault" divorce be discarded; See also J.F. Stephens, *Liberty*, *Equality*, *Fraternity*, pp. 139-145.
37. Barbara D. Whitehead and David G. Blankenhorn, p. 217; See also Lenore J. Weitzman, *The Divorce Revolution: The Unexpected Social and Economic Consequences for Women and Children in America* (New York, NY: Free Press, 1985).
38. Judith Martin, "The Oldest Virtue," in Mary A. Glendon and David Blankenhorn, *Seedbeds of Virtue: Sources of Competence, Character, & Citizenship in American Society* (Lanham, MD: Madison Books, 1995), pp. 69-70.

39. Johannes Althusius, *Politica*, pp. 29-30.
40. Michael Novak, "The Cultural Roots of Virtue and Character," in Don E. Eberly, ed., *The Content of America's Character: Recovering Civic Virtue*, p. 59.

Chapter 9

1. Leo Strauss, "Political Philosophy and the Crisis of our Time," in George J. Graham, Jr. and George W. Carey, eds., *The Post-Behavioral Era: Perspectives on Political Science*, p. 219.
2. Plato, *The Republic*, Benjamin Jowett, trans., (New York, NY: Vintage Books, 1984), Book IV; and Aristotle, *The Politics* T.J. Saunders, trans. (New York, NY: Penguin Books, 1981), Book I.
3. Alexander Hamilton, John Jay, and James Madison, *The Federalist* (Springfield, VA: Global Affairs Publishing Co., 1987), #51, p. 281.
4. Aristotle, *The Politics*, Book I.
5. *The Federalist*, p. 281.
6. Alexis de Tocqueville, *Democracy in America* (Vol. II) (New York, NY: Vintage Books, 1990), pp. 3-4.
7. Ibid., p. 45.
8. Ibid., p. 47.
9. Alexis de Tocqueville, *Democracy in America* (Vol. I) (New York, NY: Vintage Books, 1990), p. 299.
10. Leo Strauss, *Liberalism Ancient and Modern* (Ithaca, NY: Cornell University Press, 1968), p. 5.
11. John Stuart Mill, *On Liberty* (New York, NY: Penguin Books, 1988), p. 68.
12. *The Federalist*, #10, pp. 46-47.
13. Merrill D. Peterson, ed., *The Portable Thomas Jefferson* (New York, NY: Penguin Books, 1977), pp. 534-535.
14. Plato, *The Laws*, A.E. Taylor, trans. (London, U.K.: Everyman's Library, 1969), Book XII.
15. Charles S. Hyneman and Donald S. Lutz, eds., *American Political Writing during the Founding Era: 1760-1805* (Vol. I) (Indianapolis, Indiana: Liberty Fund Inc., 1983), p. 178.

16. Merrill D. Peterson, ed., *The Portable Thomas Jefferson*, pp. 334-335.
17. Alexis de Tocqueville, *Democracy in America* (Vol. I), p. 299; See also Robert Bellah, et. al, *Habits of the Heart* (Berkeley, CA: University of California Press, 1985).
18. Alexis de Tocqueville, *Democracy in America* (Vol. I), pp. 322-323.
19. Leo Strauss, *Liberalism Ancient and Modern*, p. 15.
20. David M. Ricci, *The Tragedy of Political Science: Politics, Scholarship, and Democracy* (New Haven, CT: Yale University Press, 1984), p. 304.
21. Ibid., p. 69.
22. See John W. Cooper, "Can Schools and Colleges Help Restore Citizenship?," in Don E. Eberly, ed., *Building a Community of Citizens: Civil Society in the 21st Century* (Lanham, MD: University Press of America, 1994), pp. 133-135; and Harry V. Jaffa, *Original Intent and the Framers of the Constitution* (Washington, D.C.: Regnery Publishing, Inc., 1994) pp. 23-54; Grant Reeher and Joseph Cammarano, eds., *Education for Citizenship: Ideas and Innovations in Political Learning* (Lanham, MD: Rowman & Littlefield, Inc., 1997).
23. George Anastaplo, "The Founders of Our Founders: Jerusalem, Athens, and the American Constitution," in Harry V. Jaffa, *Original Intent and the Framers of the Constitution*, p. 193.
24. Abraham Lincoln, "Address at Gettysburg" in Robert C. Baron, *Soul of America: Documenting Our Past 1492-1974* (Golden, Colorado: Fulcrum, Inc., 1989), pp. 266-267.
25. Paul Barry Clarke, *Citizenship* (London, U.K.: Pluto Press, 1994), p. 20.
26. See Plato, *The Apology of Socrates*, Benjamin Jowett, trans., (Danbury, CT: Grolier Enterprises Corp., 1980), pp. 5-30.
27. Leo Strauss, *On Tyranny* (New York, NY: The Free Press, 1991), p. 91.
28. Walter Lippmann, *The Public Philosophy* (New York, NY: Mentor Books, 1955), p. 104.

29. These are provisional proposals. Numerous universities and colleges have already developed curricula which attemrpt to fulfill the objectives of civic education within the context of the American heritage and Western traditions, particularly in General Education Programs.
30. *The Federalist*, #84, p. 465.
31. Note the judicial sanctioning of abortion and flag-burning. These examples point toward the judicial creation of special rights where none exist "by nature".
32. *The Federalist*, #84, pp. 464-465.
33. See William Golding, *Lord of the Flies* (New York, NY: A Perigee Book, 1954).
34. Leo Strauss, *Natural Right and History* (Chicago, IL: The University of Chicago Press, 1953), p. 1.

Index

About The Author

E. Robert Statham, Jr. is a Professor in the Political Science Program at the University of Guam, U.S.A. where he teaches political philosophy, American government and politics and constitutional law. He is the founder and faculty advisor of Upsilon Nu, the University of Guam chapter of Pi Sigma Alpha—The National Political Science Honor Society. Professor Statham earned a B.A. at Brigham Young University, an M.A. at California State University, and a Ph.D. at the University of Nevada.

His publications include *Between Inquiry and Advocacy: A Critique of the Pragmatic Foundations of Academic Public Policy* (1995), *Crime and the Crisis of Public Philosophy in Constitutional Orders* (1997), *Micronesian Navigational Philosophy and the Relationship Between Humanity and Nature: Etak/Itang—Where East Instructs West* (1997), *U.S. Citizenship Policy in the Territory of Guam: The Making of One Out of Many, Or Many Out of One?* (1998), and *Carl Schmitt, Leo Strauss, and Heinrich Meier: A Dialogue Within "The Hidden Dialogue"* (1998).

Professor Statham is currently researching and writing a book-length examination of United States Territorial Relations and Policy.

IRVINE SULLIVAN INGRAM LIBRARY
STATE UNIVERSITY OF WEST GEORGIA
CARROLLTON GEORGIA

IRVINE SULLIVAN INGRAM LIBRARY
STATE UNIVERSITY OF WEST GEORGIA
CARROLLTON GEORGIA